MOSCOW

AN ILLUSTRATED HISTORY

Illustrated Histories from Hippocrene

Arizona
The Celtic World
China
Cracow
Egypt
England
France
Greece
India
Ireland
Israel
Italy
Korea
London
Mexico
Paris
Poland
Poland in World War II
Romania
Russia
Sicily
Spain
Tikal
Vietnam
Wales

MOSCOW

AN ILLUSTRATED HISTORY

KATHLEEN BERTON MURRELL

HIPPOCRENE BOOKS, INC.
New York

ISBN 0-7818-0945-2

For information, address:
Hippocrene Books, Inc.
171 Madison Avenue
New York, NY 10016

Cataloging-in-Publication data available from the Library of Congress.

Printed in the United States of America.

CONTENTS

MAP x

CHRONOLOGY 1

GEOGRAPHY 11

CHAPTER 1: RISE OF MUSCOVY 13

Coming of the Slavs 13

Arrival of the Norsemen 14

The Flowering of Kiev 15

Beyond the Forests 17

Birth of Moscow 18

Mongol Invasion 20

Emergence of Muscovy 22

First Stone Buildings 24

Ivan III, the Great 27

The Kremlin 28

CHAPTER 2: MUSCOVY UNDER THE TSARS 37

Ivan IV, the Terrible 37

Division of the Kingdom 38

The Economy 41

Achievements 42

Siberian Exploration 46

Moscow in the Sixteenth Century 46

The Time of Troubles 52

The Early Romanovs 54

Schism in the Church 59

Territorial Expansion 63

The City and Patterned Architecture 64

CHAPTER 3: PETER THE GREAT AND MOSCOW'S DEMISE 69

Co-Rulers 69

Peter's Childhood 72

Moscow (Naryshkin) Baroque 73

Peter Comes of Age 74

Window on the West 75

Military Might 78

New Trends in the Arts 80

Moscow Abandoned 83

CHAPTER 4: THE AGE OF EMPRESSES: FRIVOLITY AND DILIGENCE 85
The Court Moves Back to Moscow 86
Attempt to Limit Royal Power 87
Conflagrations 89
Reign of Elizabeth 89
Rastrelli and Ukhtomsky Baroque 93
Admirer of Prussia 95
"Bloodless" Coup 98
Classical Style 102
Plague 106
Peasantry and Rebellion 108
Arts and Sciences 110
Growth of the Economy 111

CHAPTER 5: AGE OF EMPERORS: RETREAT, REVOLT, REFORM 113
Alexander I 115
Moscow Destroyed 116
Moscow Renewed 120
Decembrist Conspirators 124
Orthodoxy, Autocracy, Nationality 129
Russo-Byzantine Traditions 133
Enlargement 136
Overdue Reforms 137

Moscow's Industrial Revolution 141
The Silver Age 144

CHAPTER 6: REVOLUTIONS AND WARS 155
Grievances 155
The Revolution of 1905 159
Reaction and Neoclassicism 161
The Great War 162
The Revolutions of 1917 165
The Capital Returns to Moscow 170
Civil War 173
Bolsheviks in Moscow 174
War Communism and NEP 175
New Architecture 177

CHAPTER 7: REPRESSION AND RENEWAL 183
Rise of Stalin 183
Control of the Arts 186
The Great Terror 187
Demolition of Churches 189
Reconstruction of Moscow 190
Palace of Soviets 195
The Great Patriotic War 196

Battle for Moscow 199
The Cold War 202
Postwar Megalomania 203
Khrushchev's Ascendancy 206
Urban Expansion 209
Brezhnev and Stagnation 212
Perestroika and Glasnost 214
Collapse of Soviet Power 217
Democracy and the New Russia 221

BIBLIOGRAPHY 227

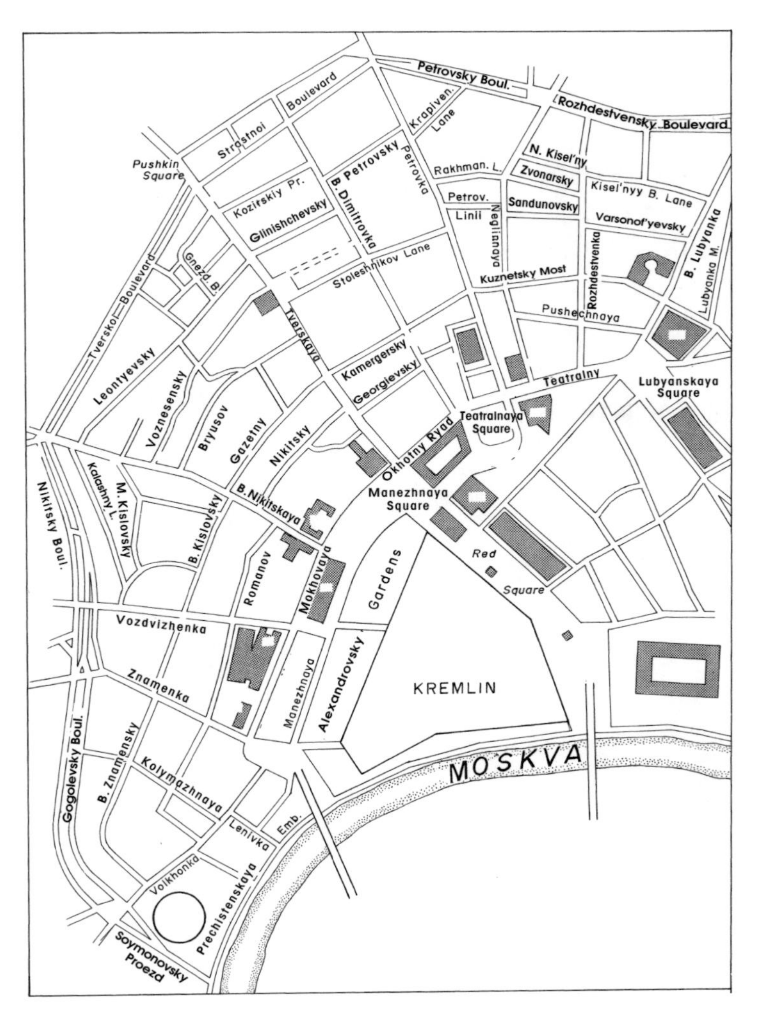

Boulevard Ring/Bely Gorod, Moscow (CREDIT: COURTNEY BOND).

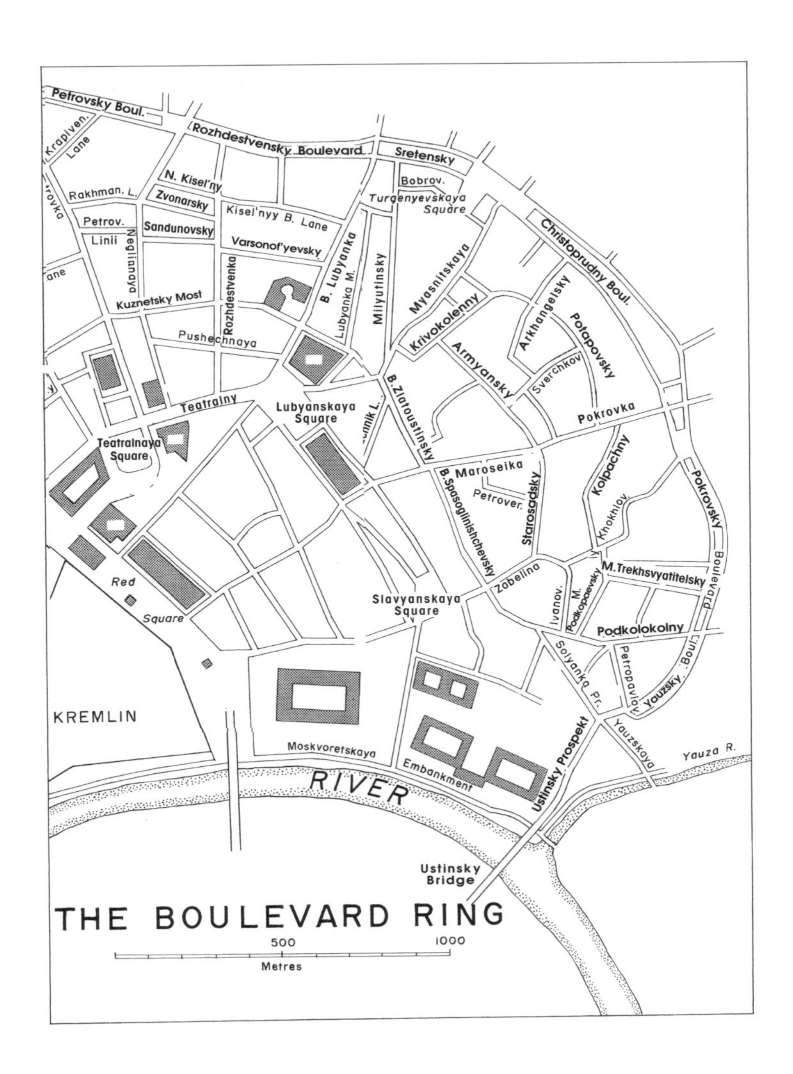

Petrovsky Boul.
Rozhdestvensky Boulevard
Sretensky
Krapiven.
Lane
Bobrov.
N. Kisel'ny
Rakhman. L.
Zvonarsky
Turgenyevskaya
Square
Kisel'nyy B. Lane
Petrov.
Linii
Sandunovsky
Neglinnaya
Varsonof'yevsky
Christoprudny Boul.
Rozhdestvenka
B. Lubyanka
Lubyanka M.
Milyutinsky
Myasnitskaya
Kuznetsky Most
Krivokolenny
Arkhangelsky
Potapovsky
Pushechnaya
Armyansky
Sverchkov
Teatralny
Lubyanskaya
Square
B. Zlatoustinsky
Pokrovka
Teatralnaya
Square
Maroseika
Kolpachny
B.Spasoglinishchevsky
Petrover.
Starosadsky
Pokrovsky
Khokhlov.
Boulevard
M. Trekhsvyatitelsky
Red
Square
Zabelina
Ivanov.
M. Podkopaevsky
Slavyanskaya
Square
Podkolokolny
Solyanka Pr.
Petropavlov.
Yauzsky Boul.
KREMLIN
Ustinsky Prospekt
Yauzskaya
Yauza R.
Moskvoretskaya
Embankment
RIVER
Ustinsky
Bridge
THE BOULEVARD RING
500
1000
Metres

CHRONOLOGY

1147 AD	Moscow is mentioned in the *Hypatian Chronicle*.
1156	Yury Dolgoruky builds the first stockade around the Kremlin.
1169	Andrey Bogolyubsky moves Rus, as the Kiev state was known, from Kiev northeast "beyond the forests."
1238	Mongol hordes under Batu Khan invade Rus and burn Moscow.
1272	Moscow becomes an independent principality under Daniel, its first prince, later grand prince.
1328–30	Stone Cathedral of the Savior *v Boru* is built in the Kremlin.
1367	The Kremlin is surrounded by stone walls.
1380	Dmitry Donskoy's troops defeat the Tatar/ Mongol forces at Kulikovo, in the first Russian victory over the invaders.
1395	The revered icon of the Virgin of Vladimir is brought to Moscow.
1422	The Cathedral of the Trinity-St. Sergius Monastery is built in stone.

1474–1508 Builders from north Italy construct the Faceted Palace, walls, bell tower, and two of the four cathedrals of the Kremlin.

1480 Ivan III refuses to pay tribute, thereby freeing Muscovy from the Tatar yoke.

1489 The Cathedral of the Annunciation in the Kremlin is completed by Russian builders.

1538 Walls are raised around Kitai-gorod east of the Kremlin.

1547 Moscow suffers a severe fire in the year of Ivan the Terrible's coronation.

1553–55 The English merchant–adventurer Richard Chancellor finds his way to Moscow from the White Sea and concludes an exclusive trade agreement with Ivan the Terrible.

1561 St. Basil's Cathedral is erected in Red Square.

1571 The Tatars under the Crimean Khan Devlet Girey sack and despoil Moscow.

1585–93 The walls of Bely Gorod, the present-day Boulevard Ring, are built.

1591 Prince Dmitry, Ivan the Terrible's son and heir, is murdered in Uglich; Boris Godunov, the future tsar, is implicated.

1591–92 Earthen ramparts and palisades are built to enclose Zemlyanoy Gorod, the present-day Sadovoe Ring.

1605–12 The Time of Troubles takes place in Muscovy.

• 1605 False Dmitry I invades Moscow with the help of Polish troops.

• 1610–12	The Poles invade again but are ousted by united Russian forces.
1613	The new Romanov dynasty begins.
1648	A new tax on salt causes riots in Moscow.
1654	Patriarch Nikon introduces reforms, leading to schism in the church.
1662	Copper coins replace the silver coins, causing serious disturbances.
1670–71	Stenka Razin leads a widespread peasant revolt.
1682	The Streltsy (musketeer guards) riot in the Kremlin.
1697–98	Peter the Great journeys to Holland and England, becoming the first tsar to travel outside his country.
Early 1700s	The first cobblestone streets are laid in Moscow.
1700–21	The Northern War between Russia and Sweden occurs.
1712	The capital is transferred from Moscow to the new city of St. Petersburg; all building in stone ceases in Moscow until 1728.
1728	Peter II moves the court to Moscow temporarily.
1730	Street lighting appears in Moscow.
1730–31	Moscow briefly becomes the capital again, when Empress Anna moves there with her court; after two years, empress and court return to St. Petersburg.
1737	Moscow suffers a disastrous fire.
1742	The Kamer–Kollezhsky Val, the customs barrier established in a rough circle beyond the Sadovoe Ring, becomes Moscow's new boundary.

1749	Prince Ukhtomsky establishes Moscow's first school of architecture.
1755	The University of Moscow is founded.
1756	*Moskovskie Vedomosti* (Moscow Gazette), Russia's first public newspaper, begins publication.
1760–70	The Apraksin–Trubetskoy mansion is built, the only example of Rastrelli baroque in Moscow.
1771	Plague devastates Moscow. Catherine II (the Great) sends her "favorite," Grigory Orlov, to quell the riots.
1773–75	The Pugachev peasant rebellion ravages the Volga lands; Pugachev is executed in Moscow.
1775–83	The royal Peter Travel Palace is built by Kazakov.
1776–85	The royal palace complex at Tsaritsyno is partially built by Bazhenov; the project is taken over by Kazakov but is never completed.
1780	The Bolshoi Theater is constructed on the present site by Michael Maddox.
1781	Water is channeled from Mytishchi to fountains in the center of Moscow.
1784–86	The Pashkov mansion by Bazhenov introduces classicism to Moscow.
1796	The first boulevard, the Tverskoy, is opened on the site of the Bely Gorod walls.

1812	Napoleon invades Russia and occupies Moscow; two-thirds of the city is destroyed by fire.
1821	The Alexandrov Gardens are planted by the Kremlin in the bed of the Neglinnaya River.
1825	The Decembrist uprising occurs.
1830	A piped water supply from the aqueduct at Mytishchi is inaugurated.
1839–80	Christ the Savior Cathedral, the memorial church to the 1812 war, is constructed.
1851	The first railway line from Moscow to St. Petersburg opens.
1853–56	The Crimean War occurs.
1861	The serfs in Russia are emancipated.
1872	Moscow Higher Women's Courses, the first institution offering higher education for women, opens.
1873	Elected local government with limited suffrage is inaugurated in Moscow.
1883	Electric street lighting commences on the Prechistenskaya Embankment.
1898	The Moscow branch of the Russian Social Democratic Labor Party, later the Bolsheviks, is founded.
1904	The Russo–Japanese War breaks out.
1905	The first Russian revolution causes loss of life in Moscow.
1914–18	The First World War takes place.

1917	The February revolution results in the overthrow of the monarchy. During the October (November 7 "new style") Revolution, Moscow sees heavy fighting and casualties. (Until 1918 Russia used the Julian Calendar, which was thirteen days behind the generally recognized Gregorian Calendar.)
1918	The Bolshevik government moves from Petrograd (St. Petersburg) back to Moscow.
1918–20	Civil war devastates the country.
1921	Famine strikes the Volga region. Lenin announces the New Economic Policy and the temporary return of limited capitalism.
1924	Lenin dies, declaring Stalin to be untrustworthy in his last testament. His body is placed in a mausoleum in Red Square. Petrograd is renamed Leningrad.
1928	First Five-Year Plan is announced.
1929	Trotsky is expelled from Russia; Stalin's rise is unopposed. Konstantin Melnikov builds his cylindrical house. Collectivization of agriculture begins.
1932	All arts organizations for writers, artists, musicians, and other creative persons are obliged to merge to form the writers' union, artists' union, composers' union, and so on.
1935	A new plan is proposed for radical reconstruction of Moscow but it is only

partially realized. The first line of the Moscow Metro opens.

1936 Le Corbusier's building for the Central Union of Consumer Societies is completed.

1937–38 This is the worst year of the Great Purge, in which millions were sent to prison camps. About eight million died.

1937–41 Construction commences for the huge Palace of Soviets, but it is never completed.

1941–45 World War II occurs. The Soviet Union is invaded by the German army, which reaches the outskirts of Moscow but is turned back.

1947 Moscow's eight-hundredth anniversary is celebrated.

1953 Stalin dies and is buried next to Lenin in the mausoleum. Khrushchev becomes the next leader of the Soviet Union. The thirty-six-story university building in Lenin Hills is completed; it is one of seven new sky-scrapers in the city in the Stalin Gothic style.

1955 The Kremlin is reopened to the public after nearly forty years.

Late 1950s Khrushchev supports rapid construction of five-story apartments to alleviate a housing crisis.

1960 Moscow's boundaries are extended, and the outer ring road is completed.

1960s–70s Prefabricated paneled housing is used to speed up construction. New "microrayons" are rapidly built up with apartment towers. Muscovites move out of the crowded city center.

1961 Yury Gagarin takes the first manned flight into space. Khrushchev openly denounces Stalin at the Twenty-second Party Congress. Stalin's body is removed from the mausoleum.

1964 Khrushchev is forced to resign. Brezhnev's rule, the "period of stagnation," begins.

1982–85 Brezhnev dies in November 1982. He is replaced by the sickly Andropov, who dies after only fifteen months. Andropov is succeeded by the aged Chernenko, who passes away a year later, in March 1985.

1985 The younger Gorbachev becomes leader. He dismisses the corrupt First Party Secretary of Moscow, Victor Grishin, and appoints reformer Boris Yeltsin.

1986 Period of *glasnost* (openness) and *perestroika* (restructuring) is inaugurated.

1991 A coup against Gorbachev is attempted by hard-liners. Yeltsin, as leader of Russia, assumes power. The Soviet Union disintegrates.

1993 Yeltsin's struggle with a reactionary parliament results in battles at the White House and Television Tower with over one hundred deaths.

1994 War begins in Chechnya.

1996	Yeltsin wins free elections.
1998	The Russian ruble crashes.
1999	Yeltsin names Vladimir Putin as his successor. A new plan for Moscow is promulgated that is sympathetic to its historic past.
2001	The Russian economy grows by 9 percent. Moscow becomes a boomtown.
2002	President Vladimir Putin and the American president George W. Bush sign the Moscow Treaty in which they agree to drastically reduce nuclear weapons.

GEOGRAPHY

Moscow, one of the world's great cities, is an island of dense urban development within an attractive, thickly wooded and watered, often swampy, region located in a central part of the vast Russian plain. This subtly undulating landscape is bordered by the taiga (with its poor soil and vast forests of pine and larch) to the north and the dry but fertile steppe land to the south. Even today, forests abound, although much forestland has been cleared for farmland and the industrial, predominantly textile, towns of modern times. The wooded, gently rolling plain crisscrossed with small and large rivers has been favorably compared with the lush countryside of New England in the United States.

Moscow's fortunes first arose because of its location at the center of the complex river systems of European Russia—those mighty waterways that were vital for communications and transportation in early times and which are still in use. Thus the small Moskva River connects with the mighty Volga, the longest river in Europe, via the Klyazma River to the north (and nowadays via the Moscow–Volga Canal) and the Oka River to the southeast. Because of this central position and the skills of its adroit grand princes, Moscow was well placed to become the preeminent town of the ancient Russian princedoms. But Russia's central plain is relatively unprotected on all sides. The Ural mountains to the east are only low-lying hills, and the Valdai hills to the north also present no real barrier. Moscow's history, therefore, is one of periodic invasion, first from the Mongols (or Tatars) in the east; then, from the west, the Lithuanian–Polish state and the Swedish, French, and (in the twentieth century) German armies.

In spite of these setbacks, Moscow was also able to continuously expand until the Soviet Union, the inheritor of the Russian/Muscovy state, disintegrated and the new Russia lost the provinces on its western and southern borders and the three Baltic states. Nevertheless, Moscow remains the capital of the largest country in the world.

CHAPTER 1

RISE OF MUSCOVY

Coming of the Slavs

The Russian and Mongolian plains witnessed a profound disturbance from the fourth to the seventh centuries as populations flowed westward out of Asia as far as Europe, overwhelming the Roman Empire and causing the disintegration of the classical world. In the seventh century, Slavic tribes—herdsmen and farmers on the edges of the Carpathian Mountains and Pripet Marshes (near present-day Poland and Belarus)—began to leave their homeland, although what precisely sparked this movement is not known. Those who went west provided the nucleus of present-day Poland, the Czech Republic, and Slovakia; others, who made their way southward, formed the core of Slovenia, Croatia, Serbia, Montenegro, Macedonia, and Bulgaria. The Eastern Slavs—the future Russians, Ukrainians, and Belorussians—settled along the mighty rivers of the broad Russian plain, displacing the nomadic and semi-nomadic tribes that had been moving about the area for over a thousand years: the Scythians, Huns, Avars, and Khazars.

Arrival of the Norsemen

The energetic Viking, or *Varangian*, Norsemen in the ninth century discovered the important trading route that linked the Baltic with the Black Sea and the glittering wealth of Byzantium via the Dnieper/Volkov and Dvina river systems. As merchant–adventurers, the Vikings quickly took advantage of this route. The independent Eastern Slav settlements, riven by internal dispute, then invited the Norsemen to be their overlords, according to the ancient *Primary Chronicle*: "Our land is great and rich but there is no order in it. Come, then to rule as princes over us." Be that as it may, in 862 the important town of Novgorod Veliky (Great) on the Volkov River was captured by Rurik, the Varangian Prince. His successor, Oleg, moved further south and in 882 took Kiev, which he made his capital.

By the time of Oleg's grandson, born in 942, the numerically superior Slavs seem to have absorbed the ruling Norse princes into their culture, for the baby was given the Slavic name of Svyatoslav. Every autumn the Norse princes collected tribute from the Slav villages and homesteads—furs, honey, wax, and also slaves—for sale in Constantinople. By a series of conquests, for a brief moment Svyatoslav's rule was vast, extending over the lands between the Volga and the Danube, north to the Finnish Gulf and Lake Ladoga near present-day St. Petersburg. In 971 his tenuous hold on these lands began to disintegrate when he was defeated by the Byzantine army. A year later he was killed in an ambush by the Pechenegs, allies of Byzantium, whose chief drank from his skull in a victory rite.

The Flowering of Kiev

Svyatoslav's son and successor, Vladimir I, transformed Kiev into a major city, which, until the middle of the eleventh century, was one of the most advanced and sophisticated states in Europe. In 988, well before the division between the Western (Roman Catholic) and Eastern (Orthodox) Churches, Vladimir adopted Christianity (his grandmother, Grand Duchess Olga, had become a Christian thirty years earlier), which put Kiev firmly within the political orbit of the western Christian nations. He chose Greek Orthodoxy of Byzantium, Kiev's great trading partner. But the beauty of the Byzantine Church also influenced Vladimir. His envoys reported as written in the *Primary Chronicle*: "We knew not whether we were in heaven or on earth. For on earth there is no such splendor or beauty and we are at a loss to describe it. We only know that God dwells there among men, and their service is fairer than the ceremonies of other nations." The church books and services had already been translated into Slavonic by Sts. Cyril and Methodius and were therefore in a tongue understood by the Kievan Russians.

Vladimir embarked on a great era of church building—by the eleventh century there were four hundred in Kiev alone. Two of the most important—the grand Sophia cathedrals of Novgorod and Kiev—are still in use for worship and even retain some of the original frescoes. Literacy also began to penetrate Slav society as manuscripts recorded church law and ritual, lives of the saints, sermons, and the first Russian chronicles. The first work of Russian literature is the outstanding epic poem, *The Song of Igor's Campaign*, written in

ST. SOPHIA OF NOVGOROD. Inspired by the Byzantine Cathedral of St. Sophia in Constantinople, this cathedral was constructed in 1045–50 for the great trading city of Novgorod. It is one of two cathedrals named Sophia—the other is in Kiev—to have survived from eleventh-century Russia.

the twelfth century and lamenting the capture of Prince Igor by the Polovtsy.

Kiev's international links are illustrated by the marriage alliances of the children of Yaroslav the Wise (1019–54). His sons took German and Polish wives; his daughters—Anna, Elizabeth, and Anastasia—married the kings of France, Norway, and Hungary.

Beyond the Forests

The brilliance of Kiev began to decline with Prince Yaroslav's death in 1054. The collective leadership he bequeathed to his heirs, five sons and a grandson, proved divisive for the state. The Cumans, nomads from the East, took advantage of the situation to inflict devastating raids on the scattered communities, carrying many Russians into slavery. The Crusades also contributed to Kiev's fall. The flow of people from western Europe into the Mediterranean on their way to the Holy Land facilitated the rise of the Venetian and Genoan republics, causing the decline of the river route from the Baltic to the Black Sea via Kiev that had been inaugurated by the Norsemen three centuries earlier. The final blow was the capture of Constantinople by the Crusaders in 1203–4.

Adding to the mounting pressure on Kiev was the threat from the north where Lithuanians, Swedes, and Teutonic Knights were sharpening their lances. Thus the center of gravity of the splintering state was forced northeastward to the *zalessky* (beyond the forests) region of the upper Volga, which was inhabited by primitive Finnish tribes. The final move took place in 1169, when Prince Andrey Bogolyubsky, great-great grandson of Prince Yaroslav, sacked Kiev and transferred his court to the banks of the Klyazma River, where he made Vladimir, in the northern principality of Rostov–Suzdal, his new capital.

Birth of Moscow

Although a Slav settlement had existed since at least the late 1000s, the first mention of the tiny outpost of Moscow occurs in the *Hypatian Chronicle* for 1147. Yury Dolgoruky, the father of Andrey Bogolyubsky and the reigning prince of Suzdal in whose territory Moscow lay, is recorded as inviting his brother princes to a banquet: "Come to me, brothers, to Moscow." Dolgoruky was son of Vladimir Monomakh (grandson of Prince Yaroslav and last prince of Kiev), and most probably his second wife, the Saxon princess Gida. She was the daughter of Harold, the last Saxon king of England who was defeated by William of Normandy in 1066. In 1156 Prince Yury built the first wooden palisade and fortress on a high point overlooking the Moskva River, where the present Kremlin now stands.

The movement of the people then known collectively as Rus—the ancestors of present-day Russians, Belarussians, and Ukrainians—to the northeast, among the wooded settlements of Finnish tribes, took the eastern Slavs further from their European center. In the harsh conditions of life in the forests, rivers, and swamps, the Slavs were still unable to form a strong central state. Although Andrey Bogolyubsky made Vladimir into a splendid town with impressive stone churches embellished with sculpted figures (three of which are still standing), the inherent suspicion and disunity of the princes resulted in the brutal murder of Bogolyubsky in his own

YURY DOLGORUKY. The prince of Suzdal, Yury Dolgoruky, is credited with founding Moscow. According to the *Hypatian Chronicle*, he held a feast there in 1147, and this is the first time the name "Moscow" was recorded. To celebrate the eight-hundredth anniversary of the city, this statue was erected in 1947, replacing the Liberty Obelisk that was unveiled by Lenin in 1918.

palace. So it is not surprising that hostile forces from outside the country once again took advantage of Russian disunity.

Mongol Invasion

In the early thirteenth century a new threat began ominously moving westward from the eastern plains. Fiercely disciplined horsemen and archers, the Mongols of the Golden Horde (the last nomadic invaders from the east) easily succeeded in penetrating the fragmented Russian lands and destroying their fragile towns and villages. Among the Mongols were significant numbers of Tatars, Turkic peoples absorbed into the Horde on their way across the Asian plains. They continued westward under the inspired leadership of Batu Khan, grandson of Genghis Khan, deep into Europe. Virtually unopposed, they occupied Hungary and areas of the Danube River. Only the death of Batu Khan's uncle saved the rest of Europe, for Batu raced back to the Mongol capital, Karakorum, to ensure he would become the new khan. He then settled in Sarai, at the mouth of the Volga River near present-day Astrakhan, where he ruled his vast territory until his death in 1255.

From Sarai the Mongols demanded annual tribute and military conscription. They periodically struck at the Russian towns, leaving them to lick their wounds and revive before the next attack. But the Mongol overlords did not interfere with the Orthodox religion, and as long as the tribute was collected, Russian life continued much as before. Nevertheless, Russia's isolation from Europe was to have profound consequences. For over two hundred years Rus suffered the Tatar

BATTLE BETWEEN THE MONGOLS AND THE RUSSIANS. The Mongols under Genghis Khan and his grandson, Batu, swept over Rus in 1222 and 1237, capturing and devastating the Kiev and Vladimir princedoms. Their two-hundred-year rule severed links with the rest of Europe and severely retarded Russia's political and cultural development.

yoke, while western Europe was starting to experience the great revival of classical learning and discovery of humanism that was the Renaissance. Despite their best efforts, Russian society and culture never quite made up this vital time lag.

Emergence of Muscovy

Slowly Moscow, although nothing more than a village in 1238 when the Mongols/Tatars invaded and burned it, began to assert itself. Moscow's position on the small Moskva River places it at the geographical center of the northern river systems of the Oka and the Volga. Vigorous colonization took place along these rivers, and strings of towns spread up their tributaries. Moscow found itself at the center of this *mezhdureche* (land between the rivers), for the Moskva River flows into the Oka, which, in turn, flows into the Volga. And the northern Volga can be reached from the Moskva by using a series of portages via the Yauza, the Klyazma, and the Kama Rivers, giving Moscow easy access to the main river highways. To the north were Novgorod and Pskov, cities not devastated by the Mongols but owing tribute to them. To the northwest was the Lithuanian Polish empire, to the east were Vladimir and Suzdal, and east and south of Moscow was the threatening Mongol Horde. *Boyars* (nobles) attracted by the trading possibilities of the river routes began to settle in Moscow.

At the end of the thirteenth century, Grand Prince Daniel Alexandrovich (1261–1303) raised Muscovy (as Moscow was known until the seventeenth century) to the status of a principality. He was the youngest son of Grand Prince Alexander Nevsky of Vladimir, who in 1242 halted the advance of the

German Teutonic Knights into Russian territory from the west. In a legendary battle on the frozen Lake Preipus near Pskov, the heavily armored German knights sank and drowned, while the more lightly clad Russians escaped. (The battle is graphically depicted in the Russian film, *Alexander Nevsky*, to music by Prokofiev.)

Moscow, still a small town, gradually began to grow, partly owing to the political astuteness of its princes and partly because there were fewer Tatar raids; consequently, a slow economic recovery was initiated.

By acting as tribute-gatherers for the hated Mongols, the unscrupulous Moscow princes began to assert their authority over other princedoms, particularly in the areas to the south and west. In 1300 under Grand Prince Daniel, the territory of Muscovy was extended to include the strategic town of Kolomna, where the Moskva River flows into the Oka on its way to the Volga. By the end of Daniel's reign, the territory of Muscovy had doubled, and in 1303 under his son,Yury, the large town of Mozhaisk to the southwest had also joined the lands controlled by Moscow.

Daniel's grandson, Ivan (ruled 1325–40) nicknamed "Kalita" (moneybags) for his ability to augment the state treasury, increased this momentum, amassing lesser principalities on the Upper Volga such as Uglich, Beloozero, and Galich. Under Ivan Kalita, the right of Moscow to collect taxes for the Mongols was acknowledged, and in 1353, with the backing of the Mongols/Tatars, Ivan Kalita's son, Ivan II "Krasny" (handsome), assumed judicial authority over the other princes. Kalita's influence was further enhanced when in 1326 Metropolitan Peter, the most important church leader, transferred his See from Vladimir to Moscow. (The metropolitan was the head of the Russian Orthodox Church until 1589, when the office of patriarch was inaugurated.) The Russian Orthodox Church had been tolerated by the Tatars during their long rule and had become a symbol of unity to the population.

Further recognition of Moscow's preeminence was given in 1395 when Russia's most revered icon, the Virgin of Vladimir, was taken from the Cathedral of the Assumption in Vladimir to Moscow. It was sent to give heart to Muscovites who were expecting an attack from the feared Mongol/Tatar leader, Tamerlane, but after the arrival of the icon, the Mongol/Tatar forces suddenly turned back and the city was spared. The Virgin of Vladimir, symbolizing political and religious power, has remained in Moscow ever since.

In 1380 Ivan's son, Grand Prince Dmitry Ivanovich (ruled 1359–89), inflicted the first victory by Russian troops on the Mongol/Tatar forces at Kulikovo, southeast of Moscow where the Don River rises (hence the sobriquet Dmitry Donskoy). Although the Tatars continued periodically to ravage the Muscovy lands for another two hundred years, the Battle of Kulikovo marks the beginning of their decline.

First Stone Buildings

The first city buildings were built entirely of easily available wood. Indeed, Russians traditionally prefer wood over stone as building material, believing it to be warmer and easier to heat. In spite of the ever-present danger from fire, they continued to build their houses and lesser buildings of this material, even when stone became available. Nevertheless, by the fourteenth century, a few important buildings were being constructed of masonry. After destruction by the Tatars, the wooden walls of the roughly triangular Kremlin or fortified citadel on Borovitsky Hill overlooking the Moskva River were rebuilt in 1367 in white limestone, enclosing a territory about one-third the size of the present Kremlin.

The first stone churches appeared in the 1330s, including the venerable Cathedral of the Savior *v Boru* (in the pine wood), which survived until 1933 when Stalin ordered it demolished to be replaced by a hall for Communist Party congresses. After the arrival of Metropolitan Peter in Moscow in 1326, two monasteries, the Chudov and Voznesensky were built within the Kremlin, signifying the secular and ecclesiastical powers of the state (both these monasteries were demolished in Soviet times). Commercial and financial activities took place outside the eastern walls of the Kremlin in what later became Red Square. The Kremlin also provided refuge during Mongol/Tatar attacks, for at that time most of the city's population could be harbored within its walls.

In the fourteenth century the city expanded to the present Boulevard Ring, where three new monastery–fortresses, the Vysokopetrovsky, Rozhdestvensky, and Sretensky, acted as sentinels. Further afield, the Danilov, Andronikov, and Simonov monasteries protected the vulnerable southern and eastern flanks against Tatar attacks. The outstanding icon painter, the monk Andrey Rublev, was working in Moscow at this time in the Kremlin churches and at the Andronikov Monastery, where he was buried. (Icons are painted religious images that are highly venerated in the Orthodox Church.) Rublev also painted the iconostasis, the screen of icons before the altar (see the Assumption Cathedral under the heading

SAVIOR CATHEDRAL, ANDRONIKOV MONASTERY. This fifteenth-century cathedral is one of the oldest buildings in Moscow. The monastery, one of several that acted as fortresses protecting the city mainly from Tatar attacks, also harbored the priest and great icon painter, Andrey Rublev. In the 1930s, like so many other monasteries it was used as a prison by the Soviet secret police.

"Kremlin"), at the Trinity-St. Sergius Monastery north of Moscow and the St. Savva Storozhesky Monastery at Zvenigorod to the south. Impressive examples of his work survive in the Tretyakov Gallery in Moscow.

Ivan III, the Great

One of the most significant acts of Dmitry Donskoy's eldest son, Vasily I (ruled 1389–1425) was the endowment in 1422 with his brother Yury of the serenely beautiful Trinity Cathedral at the renowned Trinity-St. Sergius Monastery north of Moscow. It exemplified the early Moscow style—the heavy triple-bayed white stone cube with roof gables narrowing to the single, helmet-shaped dome—that can be seen in the churches beginning to be built in stone in the Moscow region in the fifteenth century.

However, at Vasily's death in 1425, a bitter civil war broke out when Prince Yury opposed the reign of Vasily's son, Vasily II. For a quarter of a century, nephews, cousins, and uncles engaged in a struggle for the throne of Muscovy, ending only with the deaths (some by poisoning), mutilation, or blinding of all concerned. To top it all, the Tatars took advantage of the turbulence to invade Moscow, laying waste once more to everything in their path. Peace was only imposed when the throne was taken by Ivan III "the Great," son of Vasily II.

Ivan's reign (ruled 1462–1505) was remarkable for its relative stability in comparison with the previous period. At last, the boyars became subservient to the grand prince, and the perennial feuding lessened. In 1480 Ivan was strong enough to challenge the Mongol/Tatar hegemony by refusing to pay the hated tribute. Furthermore, Muscovy was able to extend its rule into the Rostov and Tver principalities, as well as Yaroslavl and distant Vyatka, and even to the proud Novgorod Republic, which included the vast northern area as far as the White Sea. Ivan also managed to wrench from the Grand Duchy of Lithuania some of the former Kievan lands as far as the upper stretches of the western Dvina and Dnieper. During his reign the land of Muscovy increased fourfold.

The Kremlin

Muscovy's international status during Ivan's reign is reflected in his choice of his second wife, Sophia Paleologus, niece of the last emperor of Byzantium before it fell to the Turks in 1453. The Russian Orthodox Church, which after the fall of Constantinople declared Moscow to be the "Third Rome," the true inheritors of Byzantium, tried unsuccessfully to halt the marriage, for Sophia was Roman Catholic. Ivan, now secure at home and abroad, set out to fulfill an ambitious plan to reconstruct and expand the Kremlin. With the aid of Italian builders and craftsmen invited through his ambassadors from an Italy in the early flush of the Renaissance, the entire Kremlin was renewed. In only thirty-four years, from 1474 to 1508, its territory was enlarged by two-thirds and its walls and nearly every church, cathedral, and bell tower was newly constructed. Since that time despite periodic additions, the Kremlin has essentially remained as conceived by Ivan.

KREMLIN FROM THE MOSKVA RIVER. Originally a palisaded fortress, by the fourteenth century the Kremlin at the heart of the city was surrounded by stone walls and included the first stone churches. In the fifteenth century under Ivan III (1462–1505) it was greatly expanded and reconstructed by builders invited from Italy.

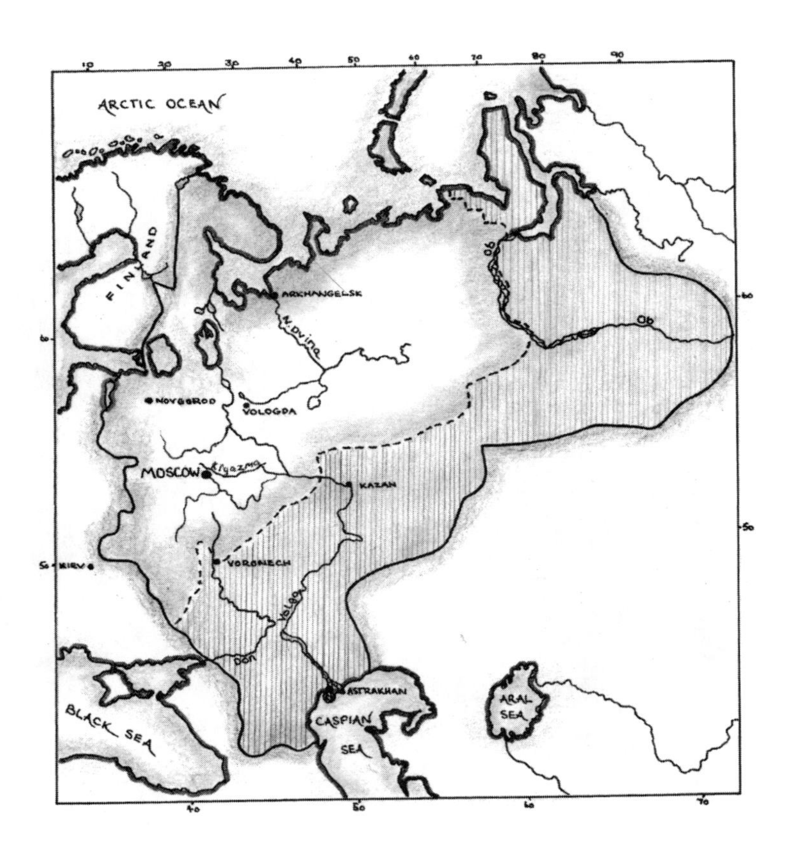

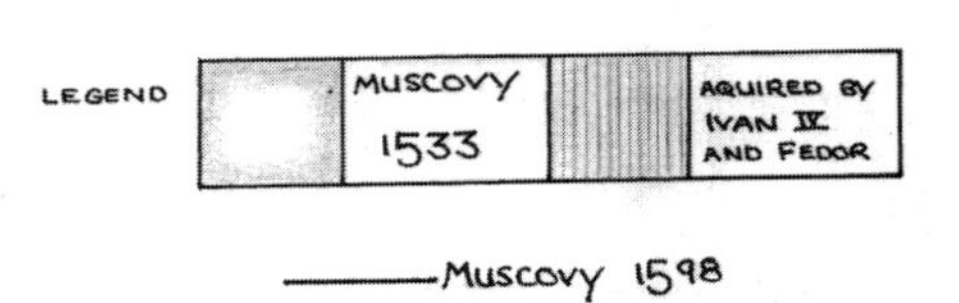

Muscovy: 1533–1598 (CREDIT: PAMELA GOODWIN)

Of the three cathedrals grouped together in Cathedral Square, the most important is the Assumption, where, until 1917, the highest state ceremonies took place, including coronations of the tsars. The Bolognese architect and engineer Alberti Fioraventi was invited to construct the church after earlier versions by Russian builders, disadvantaged by two centuries of isolation from technical improvements in Europe, had collapsed. Fioraventi, obliged to study the twelfth-century cathedral at Vladimir in order to compose a church reflecting Russian traditions and religious practices, designed a great edifice, perhaps not so large as the Byzantine-inspired cathedrals of Novgorod and Kiev but a marvelously integrated, majestic building. The Russian predilection for a bulging apse, the rounded eastern extension containing the altar, is here reduced to a barely perceptible bump, perhaps because of Fioraventi's desire for symmetry. Otherwise, it is in the Russian tradition, bearing five heavy gold-topped cupolas (domes) on massive drums (vertical supports) and the principal south facade divided into four bays, with the characteristic belt of blind arcading (arches on columns attached to a wall), slit windows, and a splendid arched portal. Inside, unlike other contemporary Russian churches, it is light and airy. Although the original fifteenth-century frescoes by the celebrated Dionisy have not survived except in fragments, the walls are completely covered with splendid seventeenth-century paintings and many ancient and valuable icons, some of which are trophies of the tsars' conquests. The tall iconostasis, the screen of icons before the altar set out in predetermined tiers, is magnificent. Large icons, including the Assumption (depicting the Virgin's body being received by heaven) for which the church is named, are grouped around the royal doors through which

ASSUMPTION CATHEDRAL, KREMLIN. This cathedral, completed in 1479, is the foremost church in Russia and is where all coronations of the tsars took place. In addition to its fine iconostasis (the screen of icons in front of the altar), it contains the most venerable icons. Until 1918 the important Virgin of Vladimir, symbol since 1395 of Moscow's preeminence and now in the Tretyakov Gallery, hung there.

the priest enters and exits. Above is the *deesis* tier, with Christ in Majesty flanked by Mary on the right and John the Baptist on the left. Radiating outward from them are the archangels and disciples. Over these large icons is the smaller row of major festivals of the church, including the nativity of Christ, the annunciation, the entry into Jerusalem, the crucifixion, the resurrection, the transfiguration, and the purification of the Virgin. The fourth tier depicts the prophets of the church and the fifth under the ceiling the Ancient of Days (the Lord Sabaoth) flanked by the patriarchs of the Old Testament.

From 1505 to 1508 the Italian Alevisio Novi rebuilt the Kremlin's second cathedral, the Archangel Michael, on the south side of the square of which the Assumption forms the head. Here he indulged in Corinthian capitals (the crowning feature of a column) and used scalloped shells for the gables, motifs that were enthusiastically copied by Russian builders. The richly ornamented west portal is like a lavish Italian doorway. This church was used as the burial place of the Moscow grand princes from the time of Ivan Kalita until the capital was moved to St. Petersburg.

The third church on the west side of the square, the royal chapel of the Kremlin, is the delightful Annunciation Cathedral with its thirteen gold cupolas. Here Italian builders were not involved; it was constructed in 1484–89 by Pskov craftsmen using the lower floor of an earlier church and was greatly extended in the sixteenth century.

The Faceted Palace (Granovitaya Palata) between the Annunciation Cathedral and the small Deposition of the Robe Church on the west side contains the audience chamber and banqueting hall of the royal palace and was the grandest building in Moscow in its time. It was built in

1487–91 by the Italians Marco Ruffo and Pietro Antonio Solario and named for the diamond pattern on the facade. It was here that Ivan the Terrible would receive delegations and ambassadors, and it continues in use today for state dinners of the Russian president.

SPASSKY GATE. The main gate linking the Kremlin to Red Square was used from the earliest times by the tsars and Soviet leaders to formally enter the Kremlin. The upper tier and cone-shaped spire (which included a clock) was added in 1625 by the English master, Christopher Galloway and the Russian, Bazhen Ogurtsov.

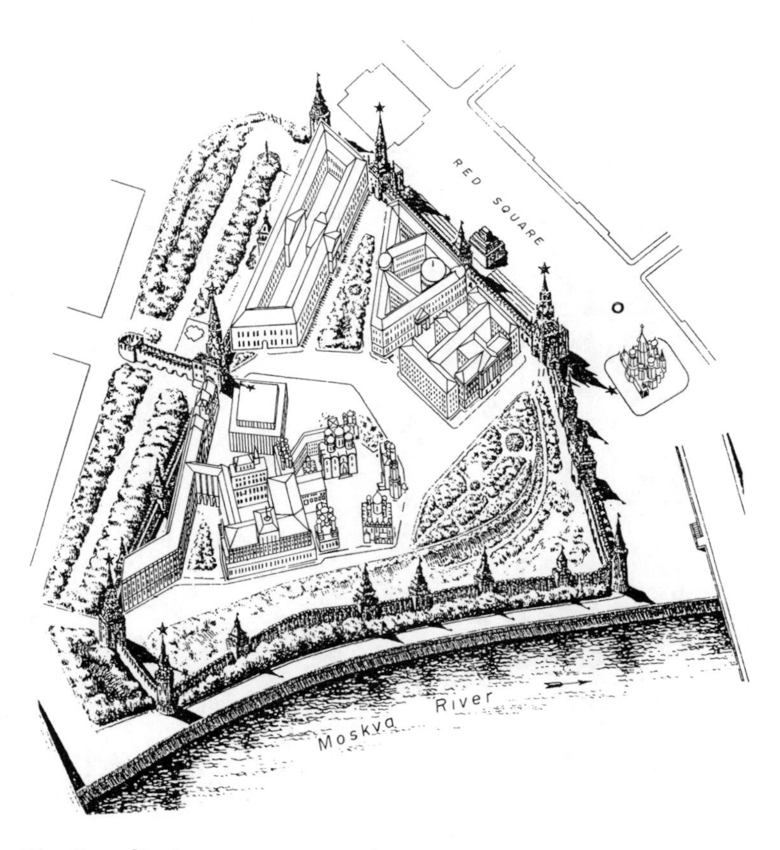

The Kremlin (CREDIT: COURTNEY BOND)

CHAPTER 2

MUSCOVY UNDER THE TSARS

Ivan III, having laid the foundations for the greatly enlarged state that now included nearly all the Russian lands, was succeeded by his son, Vasily III (ruled 1505–33). Vasily's death in 1533 left his young son, Ivan, only three years of age, under the care of the regent, his mother Yelena. Ivan's long reign (1533–84) is marked by the struggle for power between the boyars (nobles) and the tsar, which by the end had been firmly resolved in the tsar's favor. From an early age Ivan developed a strong dislike for the boyar families whose ancient feuds constantly threatened life in the Kremlin. Once the commotion even spilled over into the boy's bedroom when the metropolitan was obliged to disturb the sleeping child in order take refuge from pursuing boyars.

Ivan IV, the Terrible

In June 1547 when Ivan formally took the throne at the age of seventeen, a disastrous fire broke out in Moscow, and several thousand people died, bringing an inauspicious start to his reign. He was the first ruler officially to be designated "tsar," a corruption of "Caesar," although his father and grandfather had used the title occasionally. In that year he also married Anastasia Zakharina, a relative of the Romanovs, who were to provide the future dynasty. The marriage was a happy one, although Ivan's sadistic tendencies were already evident. On one occasion he poured burning spirits on some people near Pskov, who complained to him about a local official. The first years of his reign were also marked by military successes against the Mongol/Tatar Khanates; in 1552 he managed to take the important city of Kazan on the Volga, only five hundred miles east of Moscow. He himself took part in the fighting, along with 150,000 troops and a clever Danish engineer who succeeded in blowing up the Mongols' water supply and breaching the walls. Four years later Ivan took Astrakhan at the mouth of the Volga. This victory was an important coup for the Russians as it opened the whole course of the Volga trade to them. But the honeymoon period of Ivan's reign ended with the sudden death of Tsaritsa Anastasia in 1560 (a tsaritsa is the wife of a tsar). Ivan suspected she was poisoned by the scheming boyars, which in the atmosphere of the times was not impossible.

Division of the Kingdom

Thus the "terrible" part of Ivan's reign commenced. In his paranoia he increasingly regarded all around him with deep, sometimes justified, suspicion and retaliated cruelly and irrationally. In 1558, after obtaining Astrakhan, Ivan looked to the west to try to wrest formerly Russian lands from Livonia

IVAN IV, THE TERRIBLE. The long reign of Ivan the Terrible (1533–84) was punctuated by atrocities, diminution of the power of the boyars (nobles), and strengthening of the monarchy, but it also witnessed the great victory over the Tatars at Kazan and the introduction of the printing press.

and Poland–Lithuania. However in this he was not successful. His leading general and close associate, Prince Kurbsky, fearing the tsar's wrath for the poor performance of Russian troops under his command, fled to Poland–Lithuania in 1564. The incensed tsar had Kurbsky's family murdered and withdrew to Alexandrovskaya Sloboda northeast of Moscow, where he remained for two months.

On his return he divided Muscovy into two realms: *Oprichnina* and *Zemshchina*. Under Ivan's direct personal rule, the *Oprichnina* had as its guard a body of men selected for their loyalty and not their rank, dressed in black with the badge of a dog's head and a broom—the head for their dog-like devotion to the tsar and a broom for sweeping away treason. Their attacks on the Moscow boyars finally resulted in the loss of power and lands of this ancient nobility. Indeed, the boyars were even deprived of the right to bequeath their lands. All levels of society were now rigidly bound by ties of service—the peasantry to the nobility and the nobility to the tsar—in an inflexible structure that was not modified until the eighteenth century. In 1570 the *Oprichniki* turned their attention to Novgorod, considered by Ivan to be too independent and proud, and slaughtered more than sixty thousand people. Only a year later the Crimean Tatar Khan, Devlet Girey, led a devastating attack on Moscow with more than 120,000 men. The dispirited Russians—already suffering from the plague—could not defend themselves against such numbers, and Ivan again fled, this time to Yaroslavl to the north. Moscow was completely burned and ravaged, and many thousands of its citizens died or were taken into slavery. Nevertheless, by the end of the century the mostly wooden city had been rebuilt and enlarged.

The Economy

In other areas, important changes were occurring in the largely agricultural country. Muscovy, as a large nation-state, needed goods from other countries, and during Ivan's reign Russian merchants were more and more frequently venturing abroad for scarce commodities. Moscow, a city of one hundred thousand in the 1560s, and one of the largest European cities even exceeding the population of London (seventy-five thousand in 1550), consumed vast quantities of food that had to be delivered to its hungry citizens from the countryside. In the large country estates around Moscow, peasants began to be diverted from the land to crafts and cottage industries such as the manufacture of cloth, baskets, and farm implements. Fairs and market days were becoming popular events where goods could be exchanged, although money still was not in general use.

It was at this time that the peasants began the transition to a system in which they delivered to their lord in exchange for working his land not, as in the past, farm produce but rent money (*obrok*) and obligatory labor (*barshchina*), usually for three days a week. The villages were mostly self-supporting, although some grain was exported. This period also saw the tightening of controls by landowners over their peasants, which gradually transformed them into serfs who were completely tied to the land, but this process was not complete until the eighteenth century. The peasants were no longer able to flee at will (mostly to the open lands of the south), although on one day in the year—in November after the harvest—they were still able to leave their landowners. This, too, was completely abolished a century later. The tsar's autocratic power at the local level was still exercised by the landowners, a system that was to remain unchanged for centuries.

ACHIEVEMENTS

There were some positive aspects to Ivan's reign. In 1564 the printing press arrived in Moscow, although the printing of the first book, the *Acts of the Apostles*, caused rioting by the scribes, and it outraged Muscovites so much they chased the printer out of the city. The political scene was enlivened in 1566 by the convening of the *Zemsky Sobor*, a nascent national assembly, called by the tsar to give assent to continuing the failing war with Livonia. Its deliberations were mostly ignored by the tsar; indeed, those who complained about his repressive policies were beheaded. Renewed contact with western Europe also occurred as a natural corollary of the decline of the Tatar yoke and the expansion of Muscovy, but the important link with England happened accidentally.

English merchants were longing to find a new route to the fabled East—the spice islands of the Indies and the riches of Cathay (China) and India. To avoid the arduous and dangerous passage of the Atlantic Ocean and around the horn of Africa, it was decided to attempt another route, the northeast passage across the northern wastes of Russia to the Pacific, thence south to the exotic East. The Company of Merchant Adventurers was formed to realize these plans, and in 1553 a hopeful expedition of three sailing ships set out from Deptford near London with the blessing of King Edward VI. In the fierce winter of 1554 the ship of Sir Hugh Willoughby, the leader, foundered and became locked in ice, and all aboard perished (the remains of the ship and its log were later found).

Of the other two, only the one captained by Richard Chancellor was successful. After weathering terrible storms, it happened on the small settlement of Kholmogory near present-day Archangel in the distant north of the lands controlled by Muscovy. Here the natives suggested the English visit their tsar in far-off Moscow. The intrepid merchants aptly called "adventurers" traveled the enormous distance—about thirteen hundred miles by river—to Moscow, using the Northern Dvina and linking rivers with portages to the capital. There, after a tedious wait, they were received by the dreaded tsar himself in the Faceted Palace in the Kremlin. To their delight, they were given advantageous trading conditions, which resulted in a virtual monopoly of Russia's trade with the West for a century, until the beheading of Charles I in 1649 provided the excuse to end the arrangement. The English were pleased to outmaneuver their chief rivals, the Dutch, in this enterprise.

Although the fabled Orient was still beyond their reach, trade in timber and forest products (wax, skins, tar, hemp, and flax) for finished English goods (silks, cloth, arms, spices, lead, and copper) made quite a few fortunes in the City of London. The house the English occupied in Moscow's Kitai-gorod still stands and is considered the original English embassy in Russia. The merchants acted as the first ambassadors of the English crown to Muscovy, undertaking many commissions for Queen Elizabeth I. They also conveyed the request of Ivan the Terrible for the hand of the queen's cousin, Lady Mary Hastings. Lady Mary, horrified by rumors of Ivan's profligacy, refused the suit. Ivan's hope of an Anglo–Muscovite alliance against Poland and Sweden also came to naught, but relations between the two countries remained cordial.

FACETED PALACE INTERIOR, KREMLIN. Built by Italian builders of the late fifteenth century, this palace was where Ivan the Terrible held banquets and received foreign emissaries, including Richard Chancellor. More recently, in 1994, Boris Yeltsin hosted a grand dinner here in honor of Queen Elizabeth II on her visit to Russia.

ENGLISH EMBASSY. This residence and office of the English merchants who later formed the Muscovy Company was given to them by Ivan the Terrible after Richard Chancellor in 1553 happened upon northern Russia near Archangel while seeking a northeastern sea route to the Orient.

Siberian Exploration

After Ivan had taken Kazan, the vast expanses of Siberia and its native tribes lay open to conquest. Explorers who later took the northern routes from Vologda and Totma were greatly assisted by early penetration of these lands by Russian merchants. The most prominent were the Stroganov family, who were active in exploitation in the Urals and beyond of iron ore, copper, tin, lead, and sulfur, as well as that invaluable commodity, salt. In 1582 Yermak, the Cossack leader in the employ of the Stroganovs, captured western Siberia, including the Tatar headquarters at Sibir on the Irtysh. New towns, including Tobolsk, were quickly established in the area. (Cossacks, members of military brotherhoods, are the descendents of fugitives who fled the heavy taxes and serfdom of Muscovy to settle on the the southern frontier.)

Moscow in the Sixteenth Century

In the time of Ivan the Terrible, Moscow, although larger than London, was not as well appointed or organized. Apart from the Kremlin, it was more of a ramshackle wooden village prone to flooding, where streets could be thick with mud and where law-abiding subjects were at the mercy of bandits. It is interesting to cite the impressions of the city in the 1550s on Richard Chancellor, the first of the English merchant–adventurers, as recorded in Richard Hakluyt's *Principal Navigations, Voyages, Traffics and Discoveries*, which was first published in 1589:

> The Mosco it selfe is great: I take the whole towne to bee greater then London with the suburbes: but it is very rude and standeth without all order. Their houses are all of timber very dangerous for fire. There is a faire Castle [Kremlin], the walles whereof are of bricke, and very high . . . and on the North side there is a base towne, the which hath also a bricke wall about it, and so it joyneth with the Castle wall. The emperour lieth in the castle, wherein are nine fayre Churches.
>
> [Chancellor describes his reception by Ivan the Terrible or "the Duke."]
>
> And when the Duke was in his place appointed, the interpretour came for me into the utter chamber, where sate one hundred or moe gentlemen, all in cloth of golde very sumptuous, and from thence I came into the Counsaile chamber, where sate the Duke himselfe with his nobles which were a faire company: they sate round about the chamber on high, yet so that he himselfe sate much higher then any of his nobles in a chaire gilt, and in a long garment of beaten golde, with an emperial crowne upon his head, and a staffe of Cristall and golde in his right hand, and his other hand halfe leaning on his chaire.

During Ivan's reign, order began to extend east beyond the walled Kremlin to the Great Posad (later Kitai-gorod), which in 1538 was enclosed by strong walls by the Italian Petruchio known by the Russians as Petrok Maly. Remnants of these walls still stand. Unlike his grandfather and namesake, Ivan did not erect many buildings in the Kremlin, but

ST. BASIL'S CATHEDRAL. Although only a few buildings survived Ivan the Terrible's reign, St. Basil's, situated not in the Kremlin but in Red Square, the marketplace of the city, is truly original. Built early in Ivan's reign to celebrate the victory over the Tatars at Kazan, the cathedral has a strange and colorful design that derives from the tent-shaped tower churches. The central tower is surrounded by eight chapels of varying height to illustrate the eight attempts to take Kazan.

he did sponsor the construction of what is perhaps the most vibrant of all Russian churches. The Cathedral of the Intercession of the Virgin—or St. Basil's, as it is popularly known, after Vasily, a "holy fool" (simpleton believed to be touched by God) admired by the tsar—was built to celebrate the great victory over the Tatars at Kazan. Its eight chapels of alternating height (four small and four large), grouped around the central church, represent the eight attempts to take Kazan before the tsar's final success. Completed in 1561, it was built in Red Square, *Krasnaya Ploshchad*, the marketplace of Moscow, outside the forbidding walls of the Kremlin inhabited by the boyars whom Ivan so viscerally distrusted. (As well as "red," *krasny* also means "beautiful" or "fine"). Its bizarre, highly colored cupolas (onion-shaped domes) are the finishes to the oscillating chapels united by narrow galleries and staircases. The variety of shapes and surface patterns reminiscent of colorful Tatar carpets seem truly exotic, but its ground plan is surprisingly symmetrical. St Basil's—strange, original, magnificent—remains redolent of Ivan, who built no other church of such magnificence during his long reign.

An indigenously Russian form expressed in the core of St. Basil's is the octagonal church with its soaring tent-shaped pyramid roof. Its wooden prototype appeared in northern Russia at least as early as the thirteenth century, when it is depicted on icons. The octagonal base allowed for more spacious halls than the square-shaped cube church, for the logs used in construction were invariably cut to a standard size. As the tent-shaped tower roofs were also eight-sided, they could rise extremely high, allowing considerable internal space. The inside of the octagonal roof was usually colorfully painted with saints and archangels.

As the use of stone became more common in the sixteenth century, the tent shape was translated into masonry. The royal church at the tsars' country estate at Kolomenskoe (now within Moscow) was the first such masonry tent-shaped church in Muscovy, and some consider it to be the most elegant.

In the first half of the seventeenth century, it became fashionable to embellish these churches with a multiplicity of towers. Tent-shaped towers also appeared over gates at entrances to cities and monasteries. But this style of building survived only a century, until the 1650s, when they were banned by Patriarch Nikon in his drive to reform the Russian Orthodox Church.

By the end of the sixteenth century, Moscow had grown so much that it was encircled by its third wall after that of the Kremlin and Kitai-gorod to enclose Bely Gorod or White City ("white" meant boyars and gentry living there could be exempt from land taxes). The thick walls erected in 1585–93 by Fedor Kon extended for nearly six miles around the old center. Several established monasteries along the line of these walls provided further protection: the Sretensky, Rozhdestvensky, Vysokopetrovsky, and Alexeevsky. And further still, continuing the circular outline of the city, was the fourth boundary, Skorodom or Zemlyanoy Gorod (Earthen Town), defined by earthen ramparts and stockading built during 1591–92 along the line of the present-day Sadovoe (Garden) Ring Road.

On the extreme outskirts—in addition to the older Andronikov, Simonov, and Danilov monasteries—new fortress–monasteries and convents were built: the Novospassky, Donskoy, and Novodevichy. They further extended the defensive semicircle on the eastern and southern flanks of Moscow,

ASCENSION CHURCH AT KOLOMENSKOE. Built in 1532 on the bank of the Moskva River, the elegant tower church in the royal estate of Kolomenskoe (now part of Moscow) is an early example of northern wooden architecture translated into masonry. It was built in honor of the birth of Ivan the Terrible, who liked to spend his birthdays there. It is the prototype for the central church of St. Basil's Cathedral.

protecting the city against its most persistent enemy, the Tatars. Today, after long closure and neglect in the Soviet period, these monasteries and convents are once more bright landmarks in the city.

The Time of Troubles

In a fit of anger, Ivan lived up to his name, the Terrible, by murdering his eldest son and heir, also Ivan. In 1584 Tsar Ivan (like Stalin, with whom he is sometimes compared) died a natural death. He was succeeded by his weakly son, Fedor (ruled 1584–98). During Fedor's reign, the illiterate, wily boyar, Boris Godunov, who had risen to prominence through Ivan the Terrible's *Oprichnina,* maneuvered himself into the position of regent when Fedor married Godunov's sister. With the death of Fedor, the Rurikid dynasty that had ruled Russia for eight hundred years also came to an end. A national assembly, *Zemsky Sobor,* which included representatives of boyars, clergy, merchants, towns, and districts, was elected to choose a successor. From his powerful position Boris was able to manipulate the elections to the Assembly to ensure that he was chosen tsar. But his reign (1598–1604) was beset by deep discontents that were caused by a terrible famine, heavy taxation, and hostility to the new ruler.

Boris's unpopularity was largely due to the suspicious death of Ivan the Terrible's younger son, nine-year-old Dmitry, who was found with his throat cut in the courtyard of the royal palace in Uglich in May 1591. It was generally thought that Godunov's men had murdered him, but this was never proven. Certainly, Dmitry's death, which eliminated the leading contender for the throne, was convenient for

Godunov. Nevertheless, many Russians believed that the boy had not died at all but had fled to Poland. Thus commenced the *smutnoe vremya,* or Time of Troubles, during which no fewer than three pretenders (known as False Dmitry I, II, and III) claimed the Russian throne.

ROYAL PALACE AT UGLICH. Ivan the Terrible's son, nine-year-old Prince Dmitry, was murdered as he played outside this palace in 1591, probably by agents of Boyar Boris Godunov, who then became tsar. After Dmitry's death, a series of imposters claimed to be the prince and tried to grasp the throne, leading to the Time of Troubles at the beginning of the seventeenth century.

Godunov died a few months before the first and most successful False Dmitry entered Moscow in 1605 at the head of a Polish army, which included many disaffected Muscovites. Dmitry occupied Moscow for a year, until he was ousted by the boyar Shuisky, who then became tsar. In 1610 Shuisky was deposed by another invasion of Polish troops. In 1612 the Poles were at last expelled through the combined efforts of patriotic Russian forces led by Kozma Minin and Prince Pozharsky in which the great Trinity-St. Sergius Monastery north of Moscow played an important role. A year later a special council chose sixteen-year-old Michael Romanov (descended from the Rurikids on his mother's side and a grand nephew of Ivan the Terrible's first wife) as tsar, the first of the new Romanov dynasty.

On arrival in Moscow, the young tsar, who is reputed to have wept at the news of his appointment, complained that promises made to him that there was no more disorder in the land were false. Indeed, the Poles had not given up, for in 1618 they mounted another attack, and they were defeated only after fierce fighting and long sieges. At last, peace was obtained and a treaty was signed.

The Early Romanovs

The reign of the cautious Tsar Michael (ruled 1613–45) began full of promise after the long years of war and famine. The population had declined, perhaps by as much as a third; agricultural production had fallen sharply, only truly recovering by the 1640s; and the state coffers were empty. At first, the young tsar's mother and her Saltykov relatives were the major

TSAR MICHAEL. The first Romanov tsar (1613–45) was only sixteen years old when he hesitantly took the throne at the end of the Time of Troubles, thereby inaugurating the long dynasty that ended only when Nicholas II abdicated in 1917. Michael was a pious ruler who depended on the advice of his father, Philaret, whom he appointed patriarch and who ruled jointly with him.

influence, until in 1619 he obtained his father's release from a Polish prison, made him patriarch, and ruled jointly with him. Although they shared the title of "Great Sovereign," there seems to have been a reversal of roles: until his death in 1633, Philaret was the ruler, while his son was more interested in church matters and his great passion, flowers. Thus church and state became more intertwined than ever. In the countryside, landowners continued to gain powers over the peasants. Runaways were returned to their owners and severely punished, and landowners who employed runaways because of shortage of labor were also punished. The Zemsky Sobor, the national assembly set up by Ivan the Terrible, which sat more or less permanently and advised the tsar on various matters, could not make its decisions binding on the tsar and was unable to restrict his autocratic power.

In spite of the Polish invasion of 1618, recovery was rapid, and the city and surrounding countryside were rebuilt in an astonishingly short time. The houses and buildings, still mostly of wood, were rapidly reconstructed, as materials were easily obtained and expertise in building crafts was widely available. But wooden houses were always susceptible to the fires that were a frequent feature of Moscow life. It was at this time that stone *palata* (chambers) of the wealthy began to make their appearance, some of which with their three-foot-thick walls are still standing.

In 1635–36 Tsar Michael had a fine set of masonry chambers prepared for himself in the Kremlin: the famous Terem Palace, with its charming chapels, which rises in five tiers behind the churches in Cathedral Square. Its style is taken from traditional wooden houses, where the rooms are entered off one long porch or gallery or through a series of rooms. Its

TEREM PALACE, KREMLIN. The tiered and heavily decorated Terem Palace was built for Tsar Michael in 1636; today it is hidden behind the opulent nineteenth-century Great Kremlin Palace. The *terem*, or upper floor, was usually reserved for female relatives of the tsar.

general appearance today has only slightly altered, although inside it is decorated in the garish patterns of a nineteenth-century interpretation of traditional Russian style.

Compared to his father, who showed little interest in matters of state, Alexis (ruled 1645–76), who also took the throne at the age of sixteen, was more energetic and decisive. But he resembled his father in character, becoming known as *Tishaishy*, the Most Gentle Tsar, more kindly and humane than his predecessors, not given to excess in eating or drinking, and honorable in the observance of his marriage vows. He closely resembled his father also in his pious disposition and the hours he spent observing church rituals and services. Yet there were significant developments in Muscovy's outlook, especially toward Europe, that gained momentum in Alexis's reign.

One important change was that foreigners came to play a more important role in Muscovy affairs. Foreigners were already known to Muscovites through the Italian builders imported by Ivan III (the Great) and the foreign doctors and English traders under Ivan the Terrible. Under the first Romanovs, many more foreigners flocked to the city as specialists, providing advice on scientific, technological, and military matters. But they disturbed the hitherto unquestioned position of the Orthodox Church by practicing their own Protestant and Roman Catholic religions. Tsar Michael found contact with western ambassadors so polluting that after receiving them he would wash his hands in a golden basin beside his throne. Tsar Alexis was so shocked at their apparent impiety, the profusion of their alien prayer houses, and their lack of respect toward his person (they refused to bow to the ground when he passed) that he banished them to a special walled suburb by the narrow Yauza River on the eastern fringe of Moscow, the Foreigners' Settlement, *Nemetskaya Sloboda*. There they built fine houses and churches of various persuasions—Lutheran for the Germans and Swiss, Calvinist for the Dutch, and Catholic for others. They formed a close community, taking pleasure in discussions on the new ideas taking hold in Europe of the Reformation and Counter-Reformation.

Alexis's caution in banishing foreigners from central Moscow backfired when his young son Peter, living in the old Preobrazhenskoe Palace on the other side of the Yauza, discovered these fascinating free-thinking people and often visited them, drinking in their stories and attitudes. In this way Muscovy's interaction with western Europe, which began very slowly under Ivan III and Ivan the Terrible, began to gather momentum. Although Alexis was reputed to be of a peaceable nature, several serious upheavals occurred in his reign. In 1648 a tax on salt led to riots in Moscow, and in 1662 the replacement of silver coins by copper caused a major uprising that was brutally suppressed. In 1670 the disaffected Don Cossack, Stenka Razin, instigated a revolt among the peasantry and Bashkir, Kalmyk, and Mordvinian tribes of the lower Volga against boyars and landowners. At first successful, he was finally defeated near Simbirsk on the Volga and was brought to Moscow, where he was tortured and executed. Razin, the leader of the first major peasant rebellion in Russian history, soon became a hero of popular ballads and folklore.

Schism in the Church

It was in the middle of the seventeenth century under Tsar Alexis that the disintegration of old Muscovy became irreversible. The reactionary leadership of the boyars in their long caftans and beards was becoming less powerful, and modernizing influences from the West were beginning to creep in. But it was in the Russian Orthodox Church that the greatest upheaval was felt. Patriarch Nikon, the ambitious young cleric personally chosen by Tsar Alexis, introduced what would seem to be minor reforms in the Orthodox Church.

At first Nikon's corrections, for which he turned to the Orthodox Greeks for advice, were aimed at corruptions in Russian Orthodox practice that had crept in over the centuries. Since the fall of Constantinople and its invasion by Muslim Turks, the Russian traditionalists had considered Moscow to be the bastion of world Orthodoxy, but to the Greek prelates from Antioch and Cyprus, who were invited to advise on reform, the Moscow custom of interminable services in barely understood Church Slavonic—the ninth-century Slavic language of the prayer books and Bible, which by now was diverging from Russian—and the elaborate ritual seemed outmoded and old-fashioned. They suggested changing one letter in the spelling of the name of Jesus; crossing oneself with three fingers as in Greece instead of the Russian custom of two; and shortening some of the services. Nikon introduced these measures in 1653 and then went on to attack new trends in icon painting, even ordering the burning and destruction of offending images, which particularly angered the pious.

Church architecture, too, did not escape his reforming zeal. The indigenous Russian tent-shaped tower churches were declared to be "worldly" as they were not of Greek ancestry. He declared that churches should have one, three, or five domes and not resemble a tent. In spite of Nikon's ban, it is not recorded that any tent-shaped churches were destroyed. Indeed, bell towers continued to be built in the tent shape, and later in the same century the offending form returned in the tiered Moscow baroque churches sponsored by the Naryshkins. Nikon likewise did not approve of the so-called patterning of the many sectional asymmetrical churches with their vividly colored tiles, elaborate brickwork, and use of *kokoshniki*—the characteristic ogee (onion-shaped) gables—that were being built all over Moscow. But as his influence waned, churches also continued to be built in this style.

Nikon's policies, which had the full sanction of the tsar, led ultimately to the most devastating rupture Russian society had ever experienced. Mostly illiterate (like many of their contemporaries in western Europe), the Russian people had an unquestioning obedience to the forms of worship of the Orthodox Church, which made them reluctant to accept the changes. Nikon's insistence on the new ways, combined with his arrogant manner, merely multiplied the increasingly large number of those who adamantly refused to give up the rituals as they knew them. The country was thus riven in two and those resisting the changes—the schismatics, or Old Believers, as they were popularly known—were exiled or imprisoned. Their most charismatic leader, Archpriest Avvakum, was eventually burned at the stake, which ensured that he would become a martyr. (Avvakum's fierce and racy *Life* is one of the first examples of Russian writing using everyday language rather than the formal, difficult idioms of the church.) Old Believers stubbornly continued to resist over the centuries, and they have survived in pockets all over the country. Today, under the reforms of the new Russia, they have been given back many churches and are once more a viable community.

Nikon flaunted his power before Alexis, assuming the title of Great Sovereign as Philaret had done before him, and proceeding to interfere in both civil and church matters. Eventually, the mild-mannered Alexis had had enough and withdrew his support. Nikon retired in a huff to the fabulous New Jerusalem Resurrection Monastery he was building west

CATHEDRAL, NEW JERUSALEM RESURRECTION MONASTERY. The reforms of Nikon, the energetic patriarch, were adopted in 1654; they alienated the Old Believers and led to a ruinous schism in the Russian Orthodox Church. As he was engrossed in the construction of this fabulous monastery, loosely based on the churches of Jerusalem, Nikon so antagonized the tsar that he was tried and then exiled to the north.

of Moscow and waited in vain for the tsar to beg him to return. Instead, Nikon was ordered to appear before a court, where he was sentenced to loss of office, reduction to an ordinary monk, and exile in a monastery in the far north. The monarchy had triumphed over this serious threat to its authority by the church.

Territorial Expansion

During the Time of Troubles Muscovy lost territory in the west: Novgorod to Sweden and Smolensk to Poland. To the east, beyond the Urals, even in the Time of Troubles Muscovy continued to expand, sometimes as a result of the exploits of military adventurers. By the end of the seventeenth century, Muscovy, by subduing the local tribes, had reached the Pacific, a feat not unlike the winning of the West in America two centuries later. By 1617 the Swedes had retired from Novgorod and renounced their claim on the Muscovite throne for an indemnity of 20,000 silver rubles. As Sweden still held Estonia and other lands on the southern shores of the Baltic, Muscovy was still denied access to the Baltic Sea. Poland continued to hold Smolensk and other lands to the west, including Kiev.

In the 1650s the Cossacks in the south (Ukraine, or Little Russia), whose main interest was in preserving their military brotherhood, became worried as the Poles began extending their political and religious hold. The formation of the Uniate Church, which recognized the pope as head of the church but retained Orthodox ritual, was a blatant effort to win the allegiance of the Ukrainians. In 1651 the beleaguered Cossacks under Hetman Bogdan Khmelnitsky appealed for help to Tsar Alexis, agreeing in return that Muscovy could have suzerainty over a semi-autonomous Ukraine. Thus in 1654 Muscovy went to war against Poland. Smolensk was taken and also many Lithuanian towns, but Sweden kept Estland and Livonia (present-day Estonia and Latvia). In 1667 the Treaty of Andrussovo with Poland split Ukraine, the left bank of the Dnieper and eastern areas including Smolensk and Seversk going to Muscovy. The agreement provided that Kiev on the west bank should be part of Muscovy for only two years but it was never given up. Thus after four centuries, Kiev was once more united with the rest of the Russian people but under the control of Moscow.

The City and Patterned Architecture

If the foundations of the uniquely Russian forms in art and architecture were laid in the sixteenth century, the seventeenth saw their full flowering before Peter the Great forcibly introduced styles from western Europe. Even so, Western forms of the baroque were already beginning to creep in before Peter's time, from Poland via Kiev and from the influence of the considerable foreign community living in Moscow. Nevertheless, in the seventeenth century Russian church architecture reached heights that it never equaled again, and it is not surprising that it was to this period that the designers and architects of the late nineteenth century turned for inspiration.

In the middle of the seventeenth century the city probably had a population of about two hundred thousand, comparable to that of London. At its very center was the Kremlin, with its high walls that were fifteen feet thick in places; it was an impregnable fortress with magnificent cathedrals and palaces that had been erected by the Italians and Russians at the end of the fifteenth century. Within the Kremlin, the cathedrals high on the plateau overlooking the Moskva River were and are a splendid sight, their thirty-three gold cupolas glinting in the sun. Kitai-gorod to the east, the mercantile and market district until Soviet times, was also heavily walled. In the west the Neglinnaya River flowed along the Kremlin walls, and in the east a moat connected the Neglinnaya to the Moskva, thus ringing the roughly triangular Kremlin with water. Ivan the Terrible's colorful and splendid St. Basil's stood in Red Square next to the Kremlin. Beyond Kitai-gorod, the circular suburbs of the walled Bely Gorod and Zemlyany Gorod with their earthen ramparts and palisades made up the beautiful centripetal design of the city.

Each suburb was identified by its parish church, more and more of which were being built in stone as the local artisans—such as the cloth industry or the potters—grew in wealth. The many-sectioned asymmetrical mid-seventeenth-century churches are amazingly colorful and extravagant. They are peppered with pointed, ogee-shaped windows and gables, engaged (partly sunk into a wall) columns of many designs, as well as pierced parapets (low walls at the top of buildings) and entablatures (the decorative architectural order above the column) so that each section of wall stands out in outline, giving a bold delineation to the next level. This wild disregard for uniformity was emphasized by the lavish use of colored tiles as rich adornment. One of the most splendid is the red and white Church of the Trinity built by the rich Yaroslavl merchant, Grigory Nikitnikov, for his grand mansion in Kitai-gorod. There is hardly an inch of wall that is left free; instead, the walls serve as a background for the heavily framed windows, the columns, the rows of receding gables of the chapel and main church, and the splendid full-blown cupolas on their tall drums.

Secular buildings in stone outside the Kremlin also began to appear at this time. One that still stands is the *Krutitsky Podvore*, the residence of the metropolitans, east of the Kremlin at the crook (*krutoi*) of the Moskva River. Here the gallery, or *teremok*, connecting the chapel to the residence is completely faced with green, yellow, and brown tiles. But sumptuous buildings like these were few and far between, and nearly all of Moscow's dwellings, humble or rich, were of wood. Although they were built far apart and across ditches as precautions against fire, most, nonetheless, eventually succumbed to the frequent conflagrations and others were completely reconstructed. No wooden houses have survived from this time in their original form.

TRINITY CHURCH IN NIKITNIKOV. In the middle of the seventeenth century in the reign of Tsar Alexis, many patterned churches were built like the red and white Trinity in Kitai-gorod for a rich merchant from Yaroslavl. They could no longer be in the tent-shape form, for Patriarch Nikon had outlawed tower churches.

PETER THE GREAT. Peter's rule (1689–1725) fundamentally changed the way of life of his subjects through his energy and single-mindedness in introducing Western-based technology, fashions, and attitudes. His determination to build a new capital and port on the Baltic Sea, and to remove the entire nobility there, caused Moscow's fortunes to seriously decline, but the old capital's commercial and economic importance inevitably led to its recovery.

CHAPTER 3

PETER THE GREAT AND MOSCOW'S DEMISE

Peter was only four years old when in 1676 his father, Tsar Alexis, died and his half brother, Fedor, took the throne (ruled 1676–82). Fedor, the son of Alexis's first wife, Mariya Miloslavskaya, suffered from scurvy and died at the young age of twenty without leaving an heir. During his weak reign the scions of the two families of Alexis's wives, the Miloslavskys and the Naryshkins, vied with each other for power. At Fedor's death, his brother, Ivan, aged sixteen, would have seemed to have been the natural choice for tsar, but he was not only sickly but also feeble-witted. In contrast, Fedor and Ivan's half brother, nine-year-old Peter, was lively and healthy. Peter's mother, Natalya Naryshkina, had been the ward of the progressive Artamon Matveev, Alexis's first minister, and was brought up more freely than the secluded ladies of the *terem* (the tower or upper part of a dwelling where Russian women of wealthy or noble families were mostly confined).

Co-Rulers

The national assembly convened to consider the problem decided in favor of Peter, thus giving the Naryshkins the edge in the Kremlin stakes. But only a month later, the *streltsy*, the Moscow guards, angered by false rumors that the Tsarevich (tsar's son) Ivan had been strangled, marched on the Kremlin in their traditional caftans and rang all the bells of the city. Tsaritsa Natalya bravely stood with the children, Ivan and Peter, at the top of the Red Staircase that connected Cathedral Square to the old palace chambers, to show them there was nothing amiss. But the streltsy, their blood up, set out to murder any Naryshkins they could find, except Peter and his mother. Peter watched in horror as his uncles were thrown from the palace onto the pikes of the streltsy below and hacked to pieces. Even the tsaritsa's guardian, Artamon Matveev, was murdered. The effect on the young boy just before his tenth birthday must have been horrendous. It has been suggested that the nervous twitching of head and shoulders he suffered from later was caused by this experience.

In the end, the streltsy, exhausted by the rioting, demanded that Ivan reign as co-tsar with Peter and that twenty-four-year-old Sophia, their elder sister (Peter's half sister and a Miloslavsky), who had been released from the terem during Fedor's reign, rule as regent. The Miloslavskys were now in the ascendant. For ceremonial occasions Ivan and his half brother Peter would sit on a double throne in the Kremlin while their sister sat below, whispering advice as to how to address ambassadors and other visitors. It was immediately obvious to those present that Peter was lively and interested, Ivan still and downcast.

It is an irony that in the enclosed world of the terem where Alexis's daughters were brought up having little contact with the outside world, the eldest, Sophia, should emerge as a forceful personality—lively and energetic, relatively well educated by the standards of the day, and quite capable of

RED STAIRCASE, KREMLIN. The staircase, which gives entry to the Terem Palace ahead and the Faceted Palace on the right, is not red but white for, as with Red Square, the same word, *krasny*, means both red and beautiful. The young Peter the Great, not quite ten years old, watched with his mother from the top of the staircase as the *streltsy* (Kremlin guards) rioted, murdering nearly all his close relatives. In Soviet times, the staircase was demolished but was re-erected by President Yeltsin in 1995.

taking on affairs of the state. She took Prince Vasily Golitsyn as her lover and adviser and soon quelled the strutting streltsy by beheading their leader, Prince Khovansky. She also subjected the Old Believers to much persecution. During Sophia's regency (1682–89), expeditions mounted against the Crimean Tatars were unsuccessful, but the penetration of Siberia continued and a treaty with China was signed agreeing on the border with Russia in the Far East.

Peter's Childhood

Peter had grown up under his mother's tutelage in the ramshackle Preobrazhensky Palace in eastern Moscow, away from the dangerous court in the Kremlin. It was fortuitously situated on the Yauza River, almost opposite the enclosed Foreigners' Settlement, a district that attracted Peter as he began to come of age. Although he had a haphazard formal education, Peter liked to engage in active play, especially of war games where the soldiers would be played by the palace stable boys and his village friends. He even used real ammunition and weapons begged from the Kremlin armory, which meant that there were genuine casualties from time to time. Peter himself preferred to have the role of an enthusiastic drummer boy.

Eventually these "toy soldiers" evolved into real regiments named for the local villages, Semenovskoe and Preobrazhenskoe, which would become the most prestigious in the Russian army. Peter famously found an old English sailing dinghy abandoned in a shed at the palace at Izmailovo and taught himself to sail on local lakes. (This sailing dinghy, *botik*, known as the "grandfather of the Russian fleet," is preserved in a special museum in St. Petersburg.) Peter, who was adept at making things with his hands, enjoyed crafts like carpentry and clock making. He not only made his own shoes but even darned his stockings. His personal tastes were modest compared to earlier and later tsars, and he did not like to stand on ceremony.

Moscow (Naryshkin) Baroque

As styles from Europe began to creep into Muscovy, the delightful asymmetrical churches of the mid-seventeenth century were supplanted by a local version of the baroque, beginning in the late 1680s. This Moscow baroque—often called Naryshkin after Peter the Great's mother's family, who enthusiastically patronized the new architecture—is the first time that Russian architecture can be said to have wholeheartedly joined the mainstream of Western architectural development.

The new style used red brick as the principal material, but the string courses (horizontal bands set in walls), pilasters (a shallow column projecting slightly from a wall), columns, and, above all, the lavish window surrounds and balustrades were of contrasting white limestone. Although many churches were built in the familiar cuboid form, which supported cupolas on elongated drums and included separate bell towers, the most striking were the centralized tiered towers that rested on quatrefoil (resembling a four-leaf clover) bases. Elaborate staircases led to the first floor main church, then the building proceeded upward in a series of four-sided and octagonal tiers, one of which was open to accommodate bells, and finally terminated at the point of a single gold cupola. These "churches-under-the-bells" signaled a return to the tent shape that had been so decisively rejected by Patriarch Nikon forty years earlier. The most beautiful of these churches is surely the Intercession at Fili built by Peter the Great's uncle, Lev Naryshkin, for his estate a little southwest of old Moscow (now a factory district within the city). The Novodevichy Convent, where Peter's sister was to spend the rest of her days, also reflects the brilliant Moscow baroque style.

Peter Comes of Age

Peter was inordinately tall at six feet seven inches. He towered over his much shorter contemporaries, an awesome feature in an all-powerful tsar. However, he was odd looking with his small head and feet and narrow shoulders, and was rather ungainly. At the age of sixteen he married Yevdokiya Lopukhina, a girl chosen for him and in whom he displayed little interest. But with his marriage he became of age and tentatively began the process of easing Sophia out of power. Meanwhile the mentally deficient co-Tsar Ivan, who was no rival to Peter (he died in 1696), continued to conduct the formal duties of the office of tsar.

In August 1689 seventeen-year-old Peter took fright at the news, which turned out to be false, that the streltsy were intending to attack him at the Preobrazhenskoe Palace and rode in haste with a small band of followers to the powerful Trinity-St. Sergius Monastery, forty-five miles northwest of Moscow. There in the course of a little over a month his power grew as he was joined by sympathizers: first his mother and the patriarch, then officers, foreign soldiers of fortune, servants of the state, and finally even the streltsy. Sophia's attempts to negotiate with him failed, and in the end she was forced to resign as regent. Thus by a bloodless coup the attractive and energetic Peter (sole ruler 1689–1725) took the throne.

Window on the West

The young tsar, under the influence of his friends in the Foreigners' Settlement, such as the Swiss Franz Lefort and the old Scottish general, Patrick Gordon, turned his attention away from the ingrained habits and customs of old Muscovy to the exciting world of western Europe.

When Peter took the throne, Russia's only port was at Archangel in the far north, and it was frozen over most of the year. Interested to see the foreign ships of the English and Dutch merchants, he made the arduous journey to Archangel and himself sailed out into the White Sea. Further south he set his newly founded army (which replaced the streltsy) under Generals Gordon and Lefort against the Turks at Azov, where the Don River flows into the Azov Sea. As this attempt to gain the mouth of the Don proved unsuccessful, Peter, with the help of Dutch master builders, constructed a fleet of river galleys and barges further up the river at Voronezh. In 1696 he finally succeeded in taking the city, his first triumph, thereby marking the beginning of Russia's expansion into the Black Sea area.

Peter was a headstrong, innovative tsar, heedless of old customs and dedicated to catching up with the West, an aspiration that has moved Russia's leaders ever since. He was particularly interested in western European technical and military skills, as well as dress and social customs, but not their political institutions or civil liberties.

In 1697 at the age of twenty-five, Peter set out from Moscow for western Europe, the first tsar to go abroad. Ostensibly he traveled incognito as Peter Mikhailov, but his unusual height and large number of followers (there were 250) made his true identity obvious. Although the diplomatic aim of his "Grand Embassy" was to form an alliance with Holland and England against Turkey, he also wanted to recruit specialists and find out more about shipbuilding. After visiting the Baltic ports of Riga and Libau, he traveled via Berlin to Holland, where he remained four months working as an apprentice shipwright. He then went to England to study naval architecture. He lived in Deptford at the house of John Evelyn, the diarist, writer, and botanist, next to the Royal Dock Yard, where Peter again immersed himself in shipbuilding. Peter and his riotous entourage vandalized Evelyn's house and ruined his unique gardens by engaging in wheelbarrow races through the precious hedges and plants. To the delight of the tsar, King William not only staged a mock naval battle in his honor, in which Peter took part, but also presented him with a yacht. He took back to Russia many experts and craftsmen recruited in Holland and England, but the alliance against the Turks was not forthcoming.

In Vienna on his return journey he was informed of yet another revolt by the ever-discontented streltsy, who were inspired by rumors that Peter had died while abroad. Hoping to regain influence by restoring Sophia to the throne, they marched on Moscow in the summer of 1698. General Gordon was waiting for them and easily put the rebellion down before Peter returned. But on his arrival in August 1698 the angry tsar ordered punishment of the rebels to be renewed. In Red Square by the Kremlin walls thousands of men were flogged, broken on the wheel, roasted over fire, disemboweled, and beheaded. Peter himself, together with his favorites, took part in these cruel executions. Sophia, probably innocent of personal involvement in the uprising, was forced to take holy orders and become the nun Susanna in the Novodevichy Convent. Some of the bodies of the streltsy were strung outside her cell, where they were left hanging over the long winter. Peter's wife, Yevdokiya, was also implicated, although she seems to have been innocent, and sent to a convent in Suzdal where she was cruelly denied access to her son, Alexis.

Thus Peter's hatred of Moscow, which began with the horrors he witnessed as a boy, was intensified by this second revolt of the hated streltsy. After this he refused to live in the Kremlin, preferring for a while the run-down palace at Preobrazhenskoe, and then moving altogether to the Foreigners' Settlement, where his friend Franz Lefort had built a splendid palace.

The autocratic power of the tsar was such that he could impose foreign habits and customs on his people, which must have caused them great distress. One can imagine the scene on the day after his return from abroad. Leading boyars, who called on him to pay their respects, found the dreaded tsar bearing down on them, wielding a large pair of scissors with which he personally cut off their long and precious beards. It must have been equally painful to them to obey his order to wear Western dress instead of the long Muscovite caftans. Those who refused had to pay a special tax. Only the clergy and peasants were exempted from this law.

Military Might

After his return from his epoch-making trip to western Europe, Peter set about making many changes in Russia. He expanded the fleet through shipbuilding at Voronezh and created a modern army with the help of the many foreign advisers he had brought back with him. Once he had obtained access to the Black Sea in 1700, after his victory at Azov against the Turks, he immediately turned northward with his allies Denmark and Poland (Denmark soon withdrew) and struck at Sweden, which was blocking his ambitions to acquire a port on the Baltic. But some forty thousand Russian troops were thoroughly defeated at Narva in Estonia by the Swedes led by their young king, Charles XII.

In light of this defeat, Peter set about reforming the army. He demanded improvements in training, introduced new tactics, and began the manufacture of more modern weapons—flintlocks and bayonets and field artillery. More foreign specialists arrived. Heavy conscriptions were put on the population—one man per twenty households—and revenues from the church and elsewhere were sequestered to pay for the new army. At one time 80 percent of the income of Russia went toward the war, a heavy burden that was to provoke rebellions at inconvenient moments in Peter's various campaigns.

But Peter managed to retake Ingria as well as Dorpat and to threaten Narva. In this confident mood in 1703 he founded a fortress at the mouth of the Neva River, where it enters the Baltic on land taken from the Swedes. This was to become the graceful city of St. Petersburg. He also built the fortress of Kronstadt. Meanwhile, the Swedish forces led by King Charles negotiated a peace with the Poles and once again threatened the Russians. At first, Russian forces retreated, employing a scorched earth policy and forcing Charles to detour south via the Ukraine. The Hetman Mazeppa, the head of Cossack Ukraine, who had joined the Swedish forces proved an unreliable ally. When the Swedish army became isolated from its baggage train and munitions, the Russians struck, seizing the baggage train in October 1708. The extremely harsh winter that followed further weakened the Swedes, and on July 8, 1709, Peter's army was able to thoroughly defeat Charles at the small fortress of Poltava. In spite of this victory, the Great Northern War dragged on for twelve more years, finally coming to an end in 1721.

By the end of Peter's reign, Russia had become a major Baltic power and an important participant in the politics of northern and western Europe. His prestige was such that negotiations were inaugurated, although never concluded, for a marriage between his daughter Elizabeth and Louis XV of France. But in the south, Baku and Derbent on the Caspian Sea were lost to Persia, and Azov again reverted to the Turks (given up by Peter in 1711, when he and his army were captured by the Turks, in exchange for his freedom), thus closing the Black Sea to Russia. In the northeast, the frontiers were further extended beyond Siberia to Kamchatka and the Kurile Islands, making Russia not only a Baltic but also a Pacific power. Trade with China, largely in silk and furs, prospered.

New Trends in the Arts

European styles and fashions, grafted indiscriminately onto the Russian scene, revolutionized all the arts in the reign of Peter the Great, but they particularly affected painting and architecture. Religious painting had already been changing in the late seventeenth century as the technique of perspective was taken up by Russian artists—although not always with a sure hand—and by Peter's time, painting was ready for more fundamental innovations. For the first time, realistic portraits began to be painted of leading persons rather than the stilted iconographic portraits, *persuna*, of the early Romanovs. Roman classical myths also began to be portrayed especially in portraiture; Peter the Great is often depicted as Hercules. In the past, the Orthodox Church had discouraged three-dimensional images, although wooden religious figures had continued to be popular in the Russian north far from the central church authorities. It was only in Peter's reign that sculpture of leading citizens, with all the classical appurtenances, became popular.

In the early years of the eighteenth century, before the foundation of St. Petersburg, the new architectural style adopted in Peter's Moscow was a charming synthesis of the Western and Moscow versions of the baroque. This style was exhibited not only by churches such as the Menshikov Tower, sponsored by Peter's great friend Alexander Menshikov, but also by more practical buildings like schools, hospitals, theaters, museums, and arsenals that were built in Peter's reign. No longer (as in the past) did they all resemble each other, whatever their use; now they differed according to their function. The new architecture was based on the classical orders as interpreted by the Italian, Giacomo Vignola, whose *The Rules of the Five Orders* was translated and published three times in Peter's reign. Glass became more common, allowing windows to become larger. Brick sizes were standardized.

One of the great new buildings in Moscow erected by the wish of Peter was the impressive Sukharev Tower at the northern Yaroslavl gate, which was completed in 1701 (then destroyed in 1934). In the flamboyant Moscow baroque style, it consisted of the arched exit to the city, surmounted by two floors and a four-tiered central tower complete with clock; it was the tallest building outside of the Kremlin. Peter housed his new Mathematical and Navigational School there, the first scientific school in Russia. (At Peter's coronation, there had been only two institutions of higher learning: the recently founded Slavonic-Greek-Latin Academy in Moscow and the Kiev Academy, where the curricula resembled that of medieval grammar schools.) Staffed at first by foreigners, the Navigational School quickly expanded, and by 1712 it accommodated five hundred pupils. The first Russian sea charts were drawn there, and Russia's first observatory was placed in the upper tier by Peter's friend, James Bruce, the Russian scientist, son of a Scottish mercenary who fought for Tsar Alexis.

In 1706 Peter initiated the construction of the great arsenal in the Kremlin, but it was not completed for thirty years. It was part of his grand plan to replace the unreliable streltsy with a properly equipped modern army. Peter's governing

CHURCH OF STS. PETER AND PAUL. Peter the Great is said to have designed this charming church himself in 1705; it was completed in 1723. It is in the northern baroque manner of the new St. Petersburg but is an unusual style for Moscow.

Senate, the main administrative, legislative, and judicial body that was set up in 1711 (it lacked power, as it was completely subservient to the ruler), also had a Moscow branch, but a suitable building was not constructed until 1787 in the Kremlin. Once Peter's attention was consumed by the construction of his "paradise," St. Petersburg, where foreign builders and architects arrived in droves to create a new city on virgin ground, the old capital, Moscow, fell into a serious decline.

Moscow Abandoned

With its growth into a true, multipeopled empire, the old-fashioned appellation, Muscovy, gave way to the more modern *Rossiya*, Russia. In 1721 Peter was formally declared to be tsar and emperor of Russia, marking the great break with the medieval past. Not only was the name dropped, but also the capital was moved 450 miles northwest from the geographical center of the country to the newly founded St. Petersburg, out on a limb on the Baltic Sea. In 1712 the new northern city formally became the capital, and all the offices of state were transferred there from Moscow. The nobility were obliged to leave their comfortable Moscow homes and estates for the damp, unhealthy climate and the construction site or swamp that was then St. Petersburg. To hasten construction of the new city, it was decreed that all of Moscow's craftsmen, master builders, artists, and Kremlin artisans were to move to St. Petersburg, leaving none behind in the former capital. Building in Moscow was forbidden for many years so that all resources could be concentrated on the tsar's new capital.

It was perhaps understandable why Peter, who had grown up away from the stifling Kremlin court with its medieval customs, wanted to start afresh with a new capital, his window onto Europe, far away from the stale habits of Muscovy where so many of his relatives had been murdered. St. Petersburg was to be entirely different in character and visual aspect from patriarchal Moscow's quaint disorder. In contrast to this, the new city was to be planned, rational, a city of science and exactitude rather than the medieval jumble of leaning buildings, narrow lanes, dirt, and ignorance that was Moscow. In Pushkin's words from *The Bronze Horseman*: "Old Moscow was put in the shade by the younger capital like a purple-clad dowager by a new Tsaritsa."

By the end of Peter's reign, the country had undergone a profound transformation. No longer did the nobility—the boyars—and the people share the same culture, language, religion, and way of life. The elite were now alienated from the ordinary people, their beards shaven off, their clothes in the Western fashion; finally, as German, then French, became the language of the court, even their speech differed. Russia had expanded greatly to the west and north and had a new port on the Baltic, which connected it easily by sea to northern Europe. A new capital built on the hostile infested marshes of the Baltic by force of Peter's personality had shifted the emphasis from Moscow at the country's geographic north–south center to this ornate city on its northwestern edge. Not everyone approved. As Sacheverell Sitwell wrote in *Valse des Fleurs*, "Moscow was Russia: St Petersburg, the bastard child of Russian adultery with the manners and fashions of the West" (London: Faber & Faber, 1941).

CHAPTER 4

THE AGE OF EMPRESSES: FRIVOLITY AND DILIGENCE

Deprived of its artisans, its chancelleries, the court, and the nobles, it seemed old Moscow was left only with its commercial position intact. It never totally lost its position as a key city on the Russian scene, however, and became known as the second capital. Many nobles kept houses in both cities, for it was generally recognized that the climate in Moscow was healthier than in St. Petersburg and the land in the surrounding countryside was more productive. Coronations continued to take place in lavish traditional style in Moscow's Kremlin, and the tsars and empresses frequently paid long visits to the old city. And with time Moscow began to revive.

One important change in Peter's reign was the new law of succession under which the ruling monarch nominated the heir, rather than the old custom under which the eldest son automatically succeeded to the throne. This law had little practical effect, however, since for the rest of the eighteenth century Russian sovereigns were invariably either chosen by a cabal or installed by a coup d'etat. Nevertheless, the breakdown of tradition wrought by Peter made possible the rule of empresses for the first time in Russia. Whereas in medieval

Muscovy the only female ruler had been Sophia, the regent for the boy Tsars Peter and Ivan, Peter's death was followed by a period in which strong-willed empresses alternated with weak, short-lived emperors.

The Court Moves Back to Moscow

Peter the Great had no obvious successor. His only son, Alexis, who grew up in awe and fear of his giant, determined father, had escaped in 1717 and taken refuge in the Austrian court. The furious Peter had him tracked down, lured back to St. Petersburg, and tried in the Moscow Kremlin, where the luckless Alexis admitted that if he had become tsar he would have moved the capital back to Moscow. Peter accused his son of treason and had him thrown into the Peter and Paul fortress prison in St. Petersburg. There the terrified Alexis was slowly beaten to death, one of the most disgraceful acts of Peter's reign.

As there was no clear successor, Peter's second wife, the popular Catherine, an illiterate Lithuanian servant girl when the tsar met her, was elected by the leading dignitaries to become the first titular woman sovereign to rule Russia. She ruled as Catherine I for only two years before her death in 1727. Alexander Menshikov, the close friend of both Peter the Great and Catherine, betrothed his daughter to Catherine's successor, another Peter, son of the unfortunate Alexis and grandson of Peter the Great. But on taking the throne the eleven-year-old boy tsar (ruled 1727–30) fell out with Menshikov, sent him and his daughter into exile, and came under the sway of the conservative Dolgorukov family. The Dolgorukovs opposed the Petrine reforms and in 1728 persuaded Peter to move the court and offices of state from St. Petersburg back to the old capital, Moscow. The young tsar now became betrothed to the seventeen-year-old Dolgorukov princess, Catherine. However, on their wedding day, January 30, 1730, the bridegroom, aged only fourteen years and six months, died of smallpox in the palace of Peter the Great's friend, Franz Lefort, in Moscow's Foreigners' Settlement.

Attempt to Limit Royal Power

As there were no direct heirs and the young Peter like his grandfather had not named a successor, the Privy Council at a meeting in the Lefort Palace invited Anna Ivanovna (ruled 1730–40) to become empress. The widowed Duchess of Courland (present-day Latvia), she was the daughter of Ivan, Peter the Great's co-tsar and elder half brother, and had grown up in the royal estate of Izmailovo, now within Moscow. But the nobles who made up the Privy Council, mostly the Dolgorukovs and Golitsyns, took the opportunity to impose limitations on the powers of the new ruler, a mere woman. The provincial gentry and the influential Guards Regiments, unhappy with replacing monarchical rule with that of an oligarchy, supported Anna against restrictions on her rule, so that within the month, at her palace in the Kremlin before a gathering of nobles, she tore the document to shreds and dismissed the Privy Council. She repaid the gentry by greatly easing their obligatory terms of service from life to twenty-five years and brought in several other reforms in this vein.

Anna held court in Moscow for nearly two years, living in the wooden palace especially built for her by the great baroque architect Bartolomeo Rastrelli on the Yauza River opposite the Lefort Palace. During her stay in Moscow, street lighting in the form of glass lanterns was introduced on the main roads of the city. Her Moscow sojourn ended in the final days of 1731 when she moved to St. Petersburg, declaring she must govern "in the spirit of Peter the Great." She ruled through her German advisers, especially the baleful Ernst Biron, her lover from Courland. Biron, who did not bother to learn Russian, wielded great power over the empress, who, in effect, left all matters of government to him. He dealt with any hint of rebellion severely, no matter how highborn the offenders.

Anna's ten-year reign is remarkable for its lack of serious government and for indulgence in extravagant entertainments on which she spent over half the national income. A notorious example of her whimsy was the incomparable wedding she arranged for the court fool, Prince Mikhail Golitsyn, who was obliged to marry in the middle of winter an ugly Kalmuck woman in an ice palace on the Neva River in St. Petersburg especially erected for the purpose. Luckily, both bride and groom survived their wedding night on the frozen Neva.

It was in Anna's reign that Vitus Bering, the Danish navigator who had joined Peter the Great's navy, began the expedition that was to lead to the exploration and mapping of the northeastern Siberian coast and to the discovery that the North American and Asian lands are not joined. The Bering Straits and Bering Island are named for him.

Conflagrations

In the year 1737 devastating fires broke out in both Moscow and St. Petersburg, requiring major reconstruction in both cities. In St. Petersburg a commission under the architect Mikhail Zemtsov was set up to oversee and accelerate the reconstruction of the center on more regular lines. For Moscow, which was only beginning to revive after the removal of the capital to St. Petersburg, the fire was a terrible blow. Fortunately, the city's leading architect, Ivan Michurin, had almost completed the first detailed map of the city and had begun a comprehensive survey of its buildings, which proved invaluable in the post-fire reconstruction.

A barrier established in 1731 beyond the earthen ramparts of Zemlyanoi Gorod (the Sadovoe Ring) to control the illegal entry of vodka and wine (in the purview of the monarch) became in 1742 the Kamer–Kollezhsky Val, or general customs barrier, which hugely extended the area of the circular city. Although the collection of customs dues was abolished in 1754, the Kamer–Kollezhsky Val continued to serve as the boundary of Moscow until the beginning of the twentieth century.

Reign of Elizabeth

Empress Anna left the throne to her infant grandnephew, Ivan VI, son of her niece Anna Leopoldovna. But only thirteen months later, the baby, its mother, and their German advisers were overthrown. Elizabeth (ruled 1741–61), the capable and popular daughter of Peter the Great and Catherine, came to

EMPRESS ELIZABETH. Peter the Great's daughter (1741–61), fun-loving and capricious, was one of four strong-minded empresses who, following the reign of Peter the Great, alternated with weak emperors for the rest of the eighteenth century. She favored the florid baroque style of the gifted Bartolomeo Rastrelli, architect of the opulent Winter Palace in St. Petersburg and the Catherine Palace in Tsarskoe Selo.

the throne by means of a coup staged with the help of the French ambassador, the Marquis de la Chetardie, and the influential Guards Regiments.

The voluptuous Elizabeth, who had a stronger claim to the throne than either Anna or Ivan VI, spent her childhood and adolescent years in Moscow, away from the dangers of court intrigue in the capital. She moved to St. Petersburg in the reign of Anna but kept a low profile. In 1742 her coronation in Moscow was lavishly celebrated; in the Assumption Cathedral in the Kremlin, she placed the crown on her head herself. She declared her wish to return to the rule of Peter the Great after the excesses of Anna's reign and reinstated the Senate and other Petrine institutions, with branches in Moscow. The use of German, associated with the hated Biron, was replaced by French as the language of the court, which it remained right up to the revolution. During Elizabeth's rule of more than twenty years from 1741 to 1761, capital punishment was abolished and, less popularly, the sexes were separated in public baths. In 1754 internal customs dues were ended. This so pleased the merchants of Moscow they presented her with a great diamond and 60,000 rubles.

Fun-loving and fond of hunting and dancing, Elizabeth was at the same time pious and addicted to religious pilgrimages. Like earlier tsars she liked to make the forty-five-mile pilgrimage to the Trinity-St. Sergius Monastery northeast of Moscow. At the end of her daily walk, she would take her carriage back to Moscow or to one of the five royal palaces en route to the monastery and start again the next day at the same spot.

During her reign an attempt was made to bring order to Moscow's streets by improving lighting and regulating new

TRINITY-ST. SERGIUS MONASTERY. Founded in the fourteenth century by St. Sergius in the thick forests northeast of Moscow, this monastery became the preeminent monastery in Russia. It sent warrior-priests to the Battle of Kulikovo in 1380, resisted a long siege by the Poles in 1608–10, and harbored the young Peter while he collected forces to unseat his sister, the Regent Sophia. The ruling monarchs, especially the Empress Elizabeth, liked to make the long pilgrimage from Moscow, stopping at specially built palaces on the way.

construction. The ever-present threat of fire (two major fires occurred in 1748 and 1752) was tackled by widening the main roads to over twenty-three yards and the lanes to fourteen. This made it more difficult for fires to jump from one street to the other. Russia's first university was founded in Moscow in 1755 by Elizabeth's close confidant Ivan Shuvalov on the initiative of the great scholar Mikhail Lomonosov. A year later under the auspices of the new university, Russia's first public newspaper, *Moskovskie Vedomosti* (Moscow Gazette) began publication, ceasing only in 1917.

Elizabeth often moved the entire court from St. Petersburg to Moscow for months at a time. This greatly inconvenienced the courtiers but delighted Elizabeth. She particularly liked to hunt from her favorite Moscow residence in the suburb of Lefortovo, the former Foreigners' Settlement frequented by her father as a young man and now a fashionable district for the nobility.

Elizabeth soon acquired a lover, the Ukrainian choirboy Alexis Razumovsky, whom she probably married and by whom she may have had a daughter. As she was mostly bound up in her religious life, dancing, love affairs, and attention to her toilette (she is reputed to have had fifteen thousand dresses), affairs of state were left to capable officials. For the first time in Russian history government was conducted largely free from court interference.

Rastrelli and Ukhtomsky Baroque

It was during Elizabeth's reign that the talents of the Italian architect, Bartolomeo Rastrelli, son of Peter the Great's sculptor Carlo Rastrelli, were exploited to the full. In 1730 he became court architect to Empress Anna, for whom he built two palaces in Moscow: the wooden Winter Annenhof and Summer Annenhof, neither of which have survived. When Elizabeth ascended the throne, she found that Rastrelli's extravagant baroque style suited her fun-loving nature, and, overcoming her antipathy to the people who served Anna, she soon reappointed him court architect. His first commission was the huge and flamboyant Catherine Palace (named for Elizabeth's mother) at Tsarskoe Selo close to St. Petersburg. Rastrelli also designed private houses for the nobility and built the vivid turquoise and white Smolny Convent for Elizabeth in eastern St. Petersburg (soon to become the famous school for noble young ladies and then, in the 1917 revolution, headquarters of the Bolsheviks). Rastrelli also rebuilt the Winter Palace, now the Hermitage Museum, which with its rich color and ebullient sculptural effects, extends for thirty-seven bays along the Neva River. Ironically, Elizabeth died just as it was completed and was never to enjoy its splendor.

Although Rastrelli's Moscow palaces have not survived, the influence of his style can be seen in the fluid and extravagant lines of the Apraksin–Trubetskoy mansion (architect unknown) on Pokrovka, the fashionable street leading to the Foreigners' Settlement at Lefortovo. Built in 1760–70 and painted light green and white, with jutting oval and round halls and richly sculptured windows and cornices, there is hardly a right-angled corner in the whole of the building. Smaller and more compact than the lavish palaces of St. Petersburg, with its rounded jutting bays and heavy decoration it seemed to Muscovites to resemble a French chest of drawers—accordingly, it is known as the "house-commode."

Rastrelli's equivalent in Moscow was the baroque architect, Prince Dmitry Ukhtomsky. Most of his work is lost, like Rastrelli's Moscow buildings, but the large red and white church of St. Nikita the Martyr in Staraya Basmannaya of 1751, with its sculptural windows and soaring bell tower, is thought to be his. For Elizabeth's coronation he had designed and built four triumphal wooden arches, of which the richly detailed and gilded central arch, the *krasny* (red or beautiful), was rebuilt in stone by him and survived into the twentieth century until it was demolished by the Bolsheviks. He is also the architect of the spectacular five-tiered bell tower of the most important monastery in Russia, the Trinity-St. Sergius northeast of the city. Perhaps his most important legacy was the establishment of Moscow's first organized school of architecture, which operated from 1749 to 1764, the genesis of today's prestigious architectural school.

Admirer of Prussia

In the Seven Years' War against Frederick the Great of Prussia, Russia was just on the point of victory when Elizabeth died and her nephew, Peter the Third (1761–62), an ardent Prussian admirer, came to the throne. His first act—withdrawal from the war, thus denying Russia victory—made him fiercely unpopular.

Empress Elizabeth had arranged a marriage for him with a minor German princess, Sophia of Anhalt–Zerbst, the future Catherine the Great. In 1744, at age fourteen, she arrived in Russia. On her betrothal she took the name Catherine Alexeevna and adopted the Orthodox faith. A

KRASNYE VOROTA. One of four wooden triumphal gates in Moscow designed by Prince Ukhtomsky in the prevailing full-blown baroque style for the coronation of Elizabeth, this gate was rebuilt of masonry and survived until it was destroyed in 1928.

year later she married Peter. He was not only unattractive and extremely childish, but, according to Catherine's diaries, left the marriage unconsummated, at least for the first seven years. It was at this time that Catherine took the insignificant Sergey Saltykov as the first of many lovers, and in 1754 the heir to the throne, Paul, was born. It is uncertain whether Paul was a true Romanov, but he was accepted as such by Empress Elizabeth, who immediately snatched him away from Catherine, denying the child the care of his mother for most of his first seven years.

Although Peter's erratic and unpopular reign was short, he did accomplish one act that had far-reaching consequences. He exempted the aristocracy and gentry from all obligations of state service, except in time of war. Although this endeared him to the nobility and gentry, it released them from any obligation to serve the tsar. No longer were they required to live permanently in St. Petersburg but could return to their more comfortable estates in the lush land around Moscow, as many did for at least part of the year. Catherine was later to complain in her diary: "St. Petersburg was completely empty. Most of the well-off people lived there out of necessity but by no means at their own wish, and when the court returned from Moscow, almost all the courtiers, in order to remain in Moscow, took leave, some for a year, some for six months, some for a month or a few weeks." This led to expansion of the city in size and population and its partial renewal in the construction of many new mansions for the returning nobility.

Catherine took a new lover, Grigory Orlov, a dashing Preobrazhensky guard and one of five brothers, also members of the guards. When Catherine became pregnant by

Orlov, she went to extreme lengths to disguise it from her husband, who had also by this time found a mistress. Careful plans for the birth included orders to fire her servant's wooden house when the labor pangs began in order to distract Peter, who had always been fascinated by fires. All went according to plan: Peter rushed out to see the fire, and the baby was safely delivered and smuggled away. But relations between Peter and Catherine continued to worsen as he took to insulting and humiliating her in public. It is not surprising that plots began to form against the unpopular emperor in which Catherine was not loath to play a part.

"Bloodless" Coup

Early on June 28, 1762, while Peter was absent from the capital, Grigory Orlov's brother Alexis collected Catherine, and together they rode rapidly to St. Petersburg, where they were joined by Grigory and the famous Guards Regiments—the Izmailovsky, Semenovsky, and Preobrazhensky. The plotters encountered no opposition but only crowds of well-wishers who cheered Catherine at the Winter Palace where she appeared with her little son Paul, aged seven. When Peter heard of the coup, he attempted unsuccessfully to drum up support. At 10:00 PM on the same day (in June the sun doesn't set in this part of Russia), Catherine and her eighteen-year-old friend, Princess Catherine Dashkova, dressed in the jackets of the guards and, carrying sabers, daringly rode out from the city to the estate of Peterhof to parley with Peter. She persuaded Peter to sign an abdication order and had him moved to his estate at Ropsha under the guard of Alexis

CATHERINE THE GREAT. Born a minor German princess, Catherine (1762–96) took the throne from her unpopular, erratic husband, Peter III, with the help of officers of the guard. She reigned for thirty-four years and was known as an intelligent, sometimes wise ruler. The classical style of architecture was well suited to her habits of hard work and sensible rule.

Orlov. A few days later it was reported that he was dead, probably at the hands of Orlov and not by order of Catherine. He was the only casualty of this textbook coup d'etat.

Catherine II (ruled 1762–96) was neither a Romanov nor a Russian, yet she was enthusiastically accepted by the people of Russia as a better alternative to the pitiful, unmourned Peter. She was to prove her worth as an autocratic, occasionally wise monarch to whose name the appellation "Great" was popularly attached. She was disciplined in her work habits, rising at an early hour to study state papers, and conscientious about ceremonial occasions; she had close relations with the diplomatic corps and liked to attend plays, which she sometimes wrote herself. She bestowed great wealth and land on those who helped her take the throne. The five Orlov brothers were made counts and given vast estates in the Moscow region south of the city. One of them, the well-appointed Semenovskoe, was later used as a luxury retreat for Bolshevik leaders. Catherine's extremely lavish coronation in Moscow was celebrated with fireworks, the tossing of six hundred thousand gold coins to the crowds, and a carnival.

Catherine took a deep personal interest in architecture and embarked on extravagant building projects, some of which strained even the royal purse. Two grand palaces for her in and near Moscow were commenced but never completed, as her treasury was obliged to earmark funds for her continuing wars with Turkey. With the help of her one-time lover, Grigory Potemkin, whom she may have secretly married, Catherine extended her empire to the south along the Black Sea at the expense of Turkey. She even had dreams of taking Constantinople and had her second grandson named Constantine in the hope, unrealized, that one day he might

OTRADA, SEMENOVSKOE. Catherine gave much land to her lover, Grigory Orlov, and his four brothers in the Guards Regiments; it was the brothers' daring that had won her the throne. Vladimir Orlov's fine estate at Semenovskoe south of Moscow remained in his family until the revolution. It was then confiscated by the Soviet security services as a place of relaxation for high Communist Party grandees, including Khrushchev.

rule the old Byzantine capital. The vast new areas bordering the Black Sea, which she called New Russia, included the Crimea and gave Russia a new coastline. She toured the area in 1787, sailing with her court down the Dnieper River in huge barges, admiring the sham cottages (the famous Potemkin villages) erected along her route by her former lover to give an impression of prosperity.

Classical Style

Moscow, along with other cities and towns, changed greatly in Catherine's era. In the last quarter of the century, the strong monumental lines of the classical style had come to the fore, inspired by the fashion in western Europe, which was a result of renewed interest in ancient Greece and Rome. The empress soon came to prefer the rational lines of the classical style, unlike her predecessor, Elizabeth, who was more suited to the exuberance of the baroque. But Catherine resembled Elizabeth in that she was a great builder of palaces. She chose her architects carefully. Her favorite, the Scot Charles Cameron, confined his work to the royal palace at Tsarskoe Selo near St. Petersburg, but others, such as the Italian Giacomo Quarenghi and the Russians Vasily Bazhenov and Matvey Kazakov, built large mansions and public buildings in Moscow, some of which survive.

One of her more outlandish ideas was the plan under the aegis of Bazhenov to redesign the Kremlin by enclosing all the medieval palaces and grand cathedrals within a sweeping edifice of columns and porticoes. Although the Kremlin wall was partially removed in 1772 to allow building to commence and the foundations were laid, the grand project had to be abandoned after three years when, with the Pugachev rebellion sweeping the Volga area, the empress seemed to have lost interest in the project. In 1775 Bazhenov was placed in charge of another project for the empress, a huge sprawling complex of palaces and other buildings on the outskirts of Moscow at Tsaritsyno in the fashionable "Moorish-Gothic" style. But after ten years of work at Tsaritsyno, the empress became disillusioned when she discovered Bazhenov had become a freemason and he was peremptorily dismissed. (The empress was strongly against secret societies like freemasonry, which had become popular among the nobility in Russia in the eighteenth century.) Matvey Kazakov was then appointed, but sufficient funds were lacking, and the red and white buildings were never completed.

Although the opera house and grand palace have received attention in recent years, the attractive unused buildings of Tsaritsyno still provide the focus in the large park, a favorite place for Muscovites to relax. The brilliant Bazhenov, alienated from the court, remained in Moscow, surviving on private commissions such as the fine Pashkov House, now part of the Russian State Library, which faces the Kremlin from a height above the Moscow River. He also designed several unusual churches, some in the fashionable Gothic style, for estates of the nobility in the Moscow region.

Kazakov, who unlike Bazhenov did not study in St. Petersburg or abroad, made his very successful career solely in Moscow. He built the Peter Travel Palace in 1775–83 on the St. Petersburg road in the peculiar Gothic and traditional Russian style as a place for the empress to rest and change after the long journey from the capital. But Kazakov became

TSARITSYNO. Catherine's sprawling Gothic palace at Tsaritsyno in southern Moscow, including the figured gate and opera house, remains an attractive ruin. It was never completed, owing to the drain on the royal purse from the war with Turkey.

best known for the elegant ochre-colored classical mansions he built for the newly returned nobility and for new equally palatial public buildings. To Kazakov, the chief protagonist of this early classical period, are ascribed thirty serenely beautiful, well-composed buildings. He died a bitter man in 1813, after having witnessed the Napoleonic invasion and the destruction of Moscow.

Although Moscow was still a great village surrounded by smaller hamlets at the beginning of the eighteenth century, by the end its picturesque chambers, decorated wooden houses, and red and white sculptured churches were being offset by the ochre-colored columns and pediments (triangular gable above a door or window) and symmetrical features of the more sober classical style.

With the move of the capital to the north, the city's population declined from about two hundred thousand at the beginning of the century to about 140,000 in 1725, then rose to 175,000 in 1790. It was only in 1812, just before the Napoleonic invasion, that the 1700 figure was exceeded (251,000). Like other cities, Moscow was subjected to the new town planning regulations of Catherine's reign. Some of the curving crooked streets were straightened and paved, and suggestions were made that tree-lined boulevards should replace the crumbling circular walls of Bely Gorod, although this was not accomplished for another fifty years.

After the plague of 1771 subsided, the nobility once again sponsored the building of lavish mansions in Moscow in the city's most fashionable districts, even rivaling the royal palaces. At no other time were such huge private houses built in the city. The largest and most luxurious palace–estates were erected outside the now neglected Kremlin, like Bazhenov's imposing Pashkov house and Kazakov's Dolgorukov mansion (later the Noble's Club—its Hall of Columns is now used for concerts). Fine classical buildings erected for the university, for the magnificent new hospitals, the Foundling Home, and the new round churches so secular in appearance, dominated Moscow from every side. Within the Kremlin, a handsome building with columns and pediment by Kazakov was erected to house the Senate, the rather feeble institution set up by Peter the Great.

Theater, too, came to Moscow at this time. Although wandering players had presented biblical dramas since the sixteenth century and Tsar Alexis had established a small theater for the court, the first short-lived public theater was built on Red Square in 1702. The nobility added private theaters in their large houses staffed by the more talented of their serfs, and the new Moscow University also had a student theater. But the first really professional theater, the Petrovsky, later the Bolshoi, for opera and ballet was founded by an Englishman, Michael Maddox, and opened in a specially built building in 1780 just outside the Kitai-gorod wall.

Plague

The bubonic plague that appeared in Moscow at the end of 1770 had by the spring of 1771 turned into a raging epidemic. The better off fled the city, and gradually all trade and manufacture ceased. Measures taken by the authorities to control the disease by quarantine and destruction of property incensed Muscovites, and in September, when Archbishop Ambrosy forbade the kissing of the Bogolyubsky Virgin icon

PASHKOV HOUSE. Completed in 1786 for the descendant of Peter the Great's valet, this building is one of Moscow's finest mansions, more imposing than the palaces of the Kremlin which it faces. It was built by the court architect, Vasily Bazhenov, who, after falling out of favor with Catherine, moved his practice to Moscow.

at Kitai-gorod gate, the angry crowd searched out the luckless cleric at the Donskoy Monastery and tore him limb from limb. The mob then turned on the Kremlin, but troops under Count Saltykov managed to hold it back and to capture its leaders, who were executed. Grigory Orlov was sent by Catherine to deal with the Moscow rebellion, which he did in the cruelest fashion, arresting nearly two hundred people including twelve teenagers of whom four were executed. With the approach of cold weather, the epidemic began to wane of its own accord, and by winter it was spent, but by this time it is estimated that fifty-six thousand people in the city had died from the plague.

Peasantry and Rebellion

One of the more salient feature of Catherine's reign was the tightening of the nobility's hold over the peasantry, who had since the middle of the seventeenth century become serfs, with virtually no right to leave their landlord. It is an irony that in Russia, in the course of the enlightened eighteenth century, the liberties of the peasantry, who formed the great mass of the population, were ever more reduced. The majority of the peasants were concentrated in the rich lands of central Russia, including those of the Moscow region where agriculture was successful. With the removal of the obligation for state service, the great landowners were able to spend more time on their estates, and some began to take greater interest in agriculture and bring improvements to land management.

But life for the peasant worsened considerably. The nobles had the right to inflict cruel punishments, including beatings that sometimes resulted in death (although this was frowned upon); the peasants could be sold off to other estates and separated at will from their families; they could be sent to do military service (reduced to twenty-five years) or to settlement in Siberia. From 1767 they were even forbidden from complaining to the authorities about the abuses. The nobility and gentry, however, of whom only 16 percent owned 80 percent of the peasants, were exempt from corporal punishment and could not, according to the 1785 Nobleman's Charter, be dispossessed of their property or title without trial. Meanwhile the peasants continued to work the landlord's land at least three days a week and to pay him a heavy rent for the land they worked themselves. On top of this, they were subject to heavy taxes of about 12 percent. In times of famine or natural disaster, the peasants suffered terribly, and many tried to escape to the relatively free areas in the south and far north where the land was poor and serfdom was hardly known.

The peasants' discontent erupted at last in the Pugachev Rebellion, which broke out in 1773 in the Cossack lands in the south. Their leader, Emelyan Pugachev, passed himself off as Emperor Peter III, Catherine's erstwhile husband. The revolt quickly spread along the Volga and through the Urals, joined by peasants, who were workers in the mines of the Urals, Bashkirs, and Kazakhs. Pugachev encouraged his followers to pillage and attack their former landlords, and many of the gentry and nobility were killed and their farms destroyed. The surprisingly successful rebels managed to take Kazan, killing and looting, but the regular army, away fighting the Turks in the Balkans, finally returned and quickly defeated them. Pugachev was brought in a cage to Moscow and sentenced to be publicly hanged, drawn, and quartered.

After the rebellion had been quelled, mutual trust between master and serf was destroyed and relations worsened further. The huge disparity between the French-speaking ladies and gentlemen of the upper classes, barely distinguishable from their European counterparts, and serfs tied by bondage to their landlords was to be, as the writer Alexander Radishchev warned, the main obstacle to Russia's future progress. A cowed, illiterate peasantry would not be able to adapt easily to advances in technology or political liberties without an upheaval.

Arts and Sciences

Russia had made remarkable progress in the sciences and the arts since the reign of Elizabeth. New interest arose in the study of Russian history when the geographer and administrator, Vasily Tatishchev, who had served in Peter the Great's Swedish campaigns, retired to his estate at Boldino just north of Moscow in 1745 and wrote the scholarly *History of Russia,* which was published in the 1760s–70s. This was to be an important tool for future writers like Karamzin and Pushkin. Alexander Radishchev, an admirer of the French Revolution, wrote *A Journey from Petersburg to Moscow,* attacking the terrible state of affairs found in the serf villages along the route between the two sophisticated capitals. Sentenced to death for his writing, he was reprieved and exiled, then released, by Catherine's son, Paul I, and eventually completely rehabilitated.

Although Catherine herself encouraged satirical journals on the English model, she did not like it when writers went too far, and Nikolay Novikov, the publisher, who produced and wrote journals of a more serious kind even daring to attack serfdom, incurred her special ire. Frightened by the excesses of the French Revolution, she had him arrested in 1791 at his estate, Avdotino, south of Moscow, where he had built model houses for his peasants and provided a school and library. Like Radishchev, he was released by Paul in 1796.

The greatest scientist of the age was undoubtedly the polymath, Mikhail Lomonosov, born the son of a humble fisherman. He anticipated the atomic theory of the structure of matter and was a fine poet and philologist. Although he later lived and worked in St. Petersburg, he had studied at the Slavonic–Greek–Latin Academy, Moscow's first secondary school established in 1682 in the Zaikonospassky Monastery. It was at Lomonosov's suggestion, realized by Ivan Shuvalov, that Moscow University, which now bears Lomonosov's name, was established.

Growth of the Economy

Moscow and the surrounding province (*guberniya*) remained Russia's most important commercial region and shared in the nation's newfound wealth as the economy advanced steadily, reflecting growth in the textile industries of silk, linen, and wool and the mining of copper and iron. The wood-related industries continued to be an important export, providing much of the materials needed for shipbuilding for Britain's Royal Navy. Agriculture was depressed as usual, as conservative landowners were suspicious of improvements and peasant labor was notoriously inefficient. Cereal yields remained low, but animal husbandry was beginning to be more profitable. Drunkenness, encouraged by the state, which received 38 percent of its revenues from taxes on alcohol, continued to be a major problem in the Russian population as a whole, particularly in the countryside.

Moscow, which at the beginning of the eighteenth century had been the center from which all government radiated, had survived the deprivation of political power presented by the founding of St. Petersburg and was still the mercantile focus of the expanded empire which now included the Crimea and the Caucasus.

CHAPTER 5

AGE OF EMPERORS: RETREAT, REVOLT, REFORM

In the nineteenth century, Moscow found itself the second capital of a country that had become a fully fledged equal among the European nations. But this proved a disadvantage. Caught up in the political machinations to thwart the ambitions of the French, Moscow was forced to take the full brunt of the invasion of Napoleon's army in 1812. The disastrous Crimean War in the middle of the century created divisions between Russia and the West, encouraging the growth of the Slavophiles in Moscow, but also hastening the emancipation of the serfs, which was finally achieved in 1861. With the arrival of the liberated peasants in Moscow to work in the burgeoning factories, trade and industry in the city and its province, the most industrial area of the empire, expanded so much that levels of Russian production by the end of the century actually exceeded those of some of its European partners. However, the repressive political system stirred up dissent among a section of the nobility and the emerging radical intelligentsia. This dissent was to have far-reaching consequences.

ALEXANDER I. Tall and handsome, Alexander (1801–25) raised hopes for reform and good government after the instability of Paul I. But he never recovered from the feelings of guilt associated with the murder of his father, and he became more withdrawn and reactionary in the latter part of his reign.

Alexander I

Paul I (ruled 1796–1801), Catherine's son and successor, restored the principle of male primogeniture so that, unlike in the eighteenth century, the succession moved in an orderly fashion from father to son or brother. The ugly, cruel, and obsessive Paul—some thought him mad—inherited the ruling passion of his father, Peter III, for the Prussian military style, imposing harsh discipline on his sons and Guards officers. He ruled by whim: conceiving a consuming interest in the Order of the Knights of St. John of Jerusalem (rulers of Malta since 1530, conquered by Napoleon in 1798, then taken by the British), and suddenly for no obvious reason deciding to send an army to conquer India, an order countermanded by his son, Alexander, when he took the throne. Convinced that assassins were lurking everywhere, Paul had the fortified Mikhailov Castle built in Petersburg for his protection. Ironically, he had only just taken refuge in his new castle when in March 1801 his fears came true. A group of conspirators bribed their way into the building and murdered him. His son and successor, Alexander, was privy to the murder of his father, although he did not actually take part.

Paul's nine children, unlike their father, were tall and handsome, and his eldest son, Alexander I (ruled 1801–25), was the most physically pleasing. He had been educated under the influence of his formidable grandmother, who had chosen the liberal Swiss, LaHarpe, as his tutor. LaHarpe imbued his pupil with the ideas of reform and republicanism then sweeping Europe, but Alexander also had more conservative views in his makeup. The hopeful reforms tentatively introduced at the beginning of his reign, including a council of state and a constitution, were not put into practice.

His most influential minister, the reactionary and brutal Count Arakcheev, was particularly notorious for his administration of the new military–agricultural colonies of soldiers and their families, which allowed soldiers to engage in agriculture when they were not on active service. But the villages unfortunate enough to be included in the colonies were run by Arakcheev like military camps with frequent cruel punishments for the smallest misdemeanors applied to both sexes.

After 1815 Alexander became immersed in mysticism and withdrew in large part from direct government. But long before this happened, any real hope for reform was dashed by the overwhelming problems looming in the threat of France under the ambitious rule of Napoleon.

Moscow Destroyed

In 1799 after victories in Italy against the French army, the Russian army under the great General Suvorov made the famous appallingly difficult march across the Alps to join up with allied forces in Switzerland. During this cruel hike, one-third of the Russian army perished. Six years later at Austerlitz (Austria), Napoleon's forces defeated a large allied army, including a Russian contingent of ninety thousand men. In 1807 the Russians suffered further humiliation at the Battle of Friedland. Left with no alternative but to seek peace, Alexander in the same year signed the Peace of Tilsit with Napoleon on a raft in the River Neman. But the new alliance was uneasy and relations continued to deteriorate.

In 1812 Napoleon put together a huge force, the *Grande Armée,* of nearly half a million men, the largest ever assembled, and they began the historic march on Russia. They did not head toward St. Petersburg, far to the north in the Baltic, but toward Moscow, at the heart of the country. At first, the Russian forces retreated, and Napoleon, on his horse confidently named Moscow, advanced so rapidly that he took the ancient city of Smolensk only two months after crossing the Berezina, some 250 miles west of Moscow. The Russian army under the elderly but wily one-eyed Marshal Kutuzov finally stopped to face the enemy at Borodino, a village in the Moscow province near the ancient town of Mozhaisk, seventy-five miles west of the city. This tremendous battle on September 7, 1812, engaged 133,000 troops on the French side and 154,000 on the Russian (of whom 20,000 were hastily formed untrained militia). Both sides suffered huge loss of life after fifteen hours of fighting—45,000 Russian soldiers and 30,000 French perished. Tsar Alexander and Marshal Kutuzov, who were counting on the vast expanses of Russia and its extreme climate to discourage the invaders, decided to retreat and give up Moscow to the French army.

The terrified population fled the city, leaving behind only ten thousand citizens, many of French origin, to face Napoleon's army. Moscow's governor, Count Rostopchin, who fired his own estate at Voronovo south of the city to keep it from falling into the hands of the French, famously remarked to the tsar: "The emperor of Russia will always be formidable in Moscow, terrible in Kazan, and invincible in Tobolsk [Siberia]." For the French it proved a Pyrrhic victory.

The jubilant Napoleon arrived in Moscow on September 14 and settled in the Kremlin, impatiently waiting for Alexander to sue for peace. But no message arrived from the tsar. Instead, the city was set aflame, probably on the orders of the governor, and the horrified Napoleon was forced to move from the Kremlin to the safety of the Peter Travel Palace

MONUMENT AT BORODINO. In 1812 Napoleon and his army of nearly half a million men marched into Russia almost unopposed until they faced the Russian army under Kutuzov in the fields of Borodino, 75 miles west of Moscow. After a long and grueling battle, the Russians retreated, leaving Moscow open to the French.

on the outskirts. The fire burned for six days, affected nearly every district, and consumed the greater part of Moscow; of nine thousand private homes, sixty-five hundred were left in ashes. Along with the buildings, Napoleon's winter supplies also perished, and after thirty-three days the weary French were forced to abandon the hard-won city. Kutuzov and the Russian forces succeeded in cutting off the exit to the south, where the French would have found fresh food and provisions, and forced them to retreat along the devastated route by which they had entered Russia.

FIRE OF MOSCOW. The day after Napoleon and his army entered Moscow, fires broke out in the city. These fires were probably set deliberately, and they burned for six days, causing immense destruction in the mostly wooden town and compelling Napoleon to vacate the Kremlin for the Peter Travel Palace. The fire was instrumental in destroying winter supplies, thereby forcing Napoleon's early departure from Moscow only thirty-three days after he had triumphantly entered it.

The sudden drop in temperature at the onset of a particularly harsh winter, combined with constant harassment by Russian troops, decimated the once proud French army, and the dejected Napoleon recrossed the Berezina River with only one-tenth of the troops with which he had invaded Russia. The handsome Alexander at the head of his army on his horse, Eclipse, ironically a present from Napoleon in earlier times, marched triumphantly into Paris on March 19, 1814. He was not only one of the principal leaders of the coalition against Napoleon but also head of the first country to defeat him on land.

After he was finally defeated at the Battle of Waterloo, on June 18, 1815, Napoleon abdicated, and the allies, Russia among them, occupied France, albeit briefly, as the victors. At the Congress of Vienna in 1815, convened to decide the future of continental Europe, Russia played a leading role.

Moscow Renewed

An appalling sight greeted the returning Muscovites. Bodies lay everywhere on the filthy, rubble-strewn streets. Two-thirds of all the city's buildings had been destroyed or suffered extensive fire damage. Ancient libraries had gone up in smoke, and icons had burned. What had not been damaged by fire disappeared in the looting that followed. The Kremlin was particularly affected, not so much from fire but from damage by mines laid by the French before their departure. Amid the awful scenes of destruction, there was nevertheless a general feeling of euphoria that Russia had been able to vanquish the invincible Napoleon, a defeat that was decisive in his ultimate downfall.

Reconstruction became a question of national pride. A Commission for the Construction of Moscow was immediately formed to rebuild the shattered city. The tsar took a direct interest in Moscow's rebirth and personally appointed the Scot, William Hastie, designer of some of the finest iron bridges in St. Petersburg, to devise a plan for the renewal of the shattered city. Hastie's plan, blind to Moscow's historical layout, involved totally reconstructing the center by the imposition of straight streets, wide boulevards, and a series of huge linked squares. The Moscow Commission managed to ignore Hastie's more radical ideas but agreed to the new squares surrounding the Kremlin. The most imposing was Theater Square with the Bolshoi Theater at its head (rebuilt in 1824 after a fire in 1805). This adapted plan, a quarter of the cost of the Hastie scheme, left the old Kremlin at the center of the traditional radial-circular arrangement. Moscow was not to lose its original highly picturesque appearance.

Osip Bove, the chief architect appointed to oversee the reconstruction of Moscow, favored the delightful Empire form of the classical style in which elegant moldings enliven the facades, and rotundas as well as domes are prominent features. The intimate buildings are smaller and less monumental than the severe classicism of St. Petersburg. The restored private houses for the gentry, less imposing than previously, were built of brick under plaster, of two or three stories, and endowed with reliefs, wreaths, or swags (resembling draped cloth). The commission laid down strict regulations, even deciding on the colors of the roofs and the facades,

BOLSHOI THEATER. The theater for opera and masques was first built here in 1780 by an English entrepreneur, Michael Maddox. After a fire it was rebuilt in 1824 in the classical style when Osip Bove, the city architect, opened the approaches to the building by creating a large square. The theater burned down again in 1853 and was rebuilt in its final form three years later.

mostly painted in variations of ochre. Gardens belonging to each house were reinstated, giving breathing space to the streets unlike St. Petersburg with its small courtyards and severe facades flush with the street. Reconstruction was rapid; by 1816 some 72 percent of stone houses were repaired or built anew, and over half the wooden buildings and houses were restored. Public houses and squares were also built or renewed.

OLD BUILDING OF MOSCOW UNIVERSITY. Founded in 1753, the first university in Russia was designed originally in classical style by Matvey Kazakov; after the fire of Napoleon's invasion, it was rebuilt in the prevailing Empire style with attractive reliefs and moldings. In the nineteenth century Moscow University enjoyed a more radical reputation than its sister institution in St. Petersburg.

The tsar personally proposed the building of a large *manege* or exercise house for horses, alongside the Kremlin. It was completed in eight months for his visit in November 1817, but the roof over the huge interior proved inadequate and was rebuilt in 1825 by Bove, who also added the plasterwork and moldings. Red Square was widened and improved with the building of Bove's market hall; the Neglinnaya River along the Kremlin wall was rechanneled underground, and the Alexandrov Gardens were laid out in its place; and the university buildings facing the Kremlin were completely rebuilt in the Empire style.

Decembrist Conspirators

The many officers in Alexander's train on their visits to France and other west European countries were impressed at the gulf in living standards between Russia and western Europe and at the liberal and republican sentiments then in vogue, especially in France. Within Russia, many of the newly emerging intelligentsia who had never left the country were imbibing similar ideas from books and journals.

By 1820 a group of dissident army officers had emerged. Together with a few government officials and some merchants, they were inspired by the wave of patriotism brought on by the 1812 victory and by the liberal ideas of western Europe. They began forming secret societies all over the country, which became debating clubs on the best way forward for the nation. A particularly active group was located at the cavalry school for young officers in Moscow, which was run by Major General Nikolay Muraviev. In the summers the students moved to the Muraviev estate in the Moscow region west of the city at Ostashevo. The radical thinking there influenced the young of the nearby great estates—the Chernyshev, Sheremetiev, and Shakhovskoy families—making the area a veritable hotbed of dissent. Twenty-two of the cavalry school graduates were to actively engage in the Decembrist conspiracy (see the next section), as well as three of Muraviev's five sons and the young nobles of the neighboring estates.

STABLES AT OSTASHEVO. Nikolay Muraviev's elite cavalry school moved in the summers to his country estate, Ostashevo, west of Moscow where secret meetings could be held far from prying eyes. Twenty-two of his students were to become rebels, the Decembrists, who staged the failed insurrection against the monarchy that ushered in the reign of Nicholas I (1825–55).

On learning of these young political radicals, many of them from aristocratic families, Tsar Alexander regarded them at first benignly, stating that they were only expressing the kind of opinions he had held in his youth. Some were republicans in favor of doing away with the monarchy altogether, while others advocated some form of constitutional monarchy, and still others were intent on abolishing serfdom—but there was a general consensus on the need for reform and limitations on the powers of the autocracy. One of their plans was to assassinate the tsar in May 1826. But this plot was preempted by his unexpected death in November 1825 from typhoid in Taganrog on the Sea of Azov in southern Russia.

As Alexander had no sons, the heir to the throne was automatically his brother Constantine. But Constantine, commander in chief of the Russian Army in Poland, had some years before informed Alexander that he wished to renounce the succession. Alexander agreed, naming their younger brother, Nicholas, successor but he kept this information so secret that, on hearing of the tsar's death, Nicholas immediately swore allegiance to Constantine.

It was not until after nearly three weeks, in December (therefore the appellation, Decembrists) that Nicholas claimed the crown. The Senate (the administrative, legislative, and judicial body subordinate to the tsar) and the Holy Synod (in charge of religious affairs) complied immediately, but the required oath of allegiance of the Guards Regiments of St. Petersburg did not come easily. On December 14, the swearing-in commenced, but soon mutinies began to break out and some two thousand officers and men marched to Senate Square west of the Winter Palace. Although the officers were aware of the reasons they were there, their men were not so sure and when they cheered for "Konstantin i Konstitutsia [Constitution]," they thought it meant Constantine and his wife.

Nicholas attempted to persuade the rebels to surrender, but after several hours in sub-zero weather, he ordered cannon fire to be opened up on the rebels. At least fifty died in the square, and others perished as the ice gave way on the Neva River under their horses' hoofs. Nicholas himself interrogated the prisoners. Five were hanged, including the leaders Colonel Pestel and the poet Ryleev. But, typically, the execution on July 13, 1826, at the Peter and Paul fortress was bungled so badly that one of the victims whose legs were broken in the first attempt famously declared, "They can't even hang a man decently in Russia."

Over one hundred officers were exiled to Siberia, where these sons of the nobility were employed in the harsh conditions of the mines. They were first taken to Moscow, and from there they set out on foot along the Vladimirka, the dismal long road east. At the first post house, Gorenky (from *gore* meaning grief), families were allowed to bid farewell to the prisoners, whom they might never see again. Some of the more intrepid of the Decembrists' wives also made the long journey to be with their husbands—for which they had to have the tsar's permission—to be faced with conditions more primitive than they ever could have imagined. Before the Decembrist uprising the great Russian poet, Alexander Pushkin, had been exiled for his inflammatory verse to his estate and, fortunately for Russian literature, had been unable to participate in the revolt with which he had great sympathy. But at a gathering at Princess Zinaida Volkonskaya's fine

ALEXANDER PUSHKIN. The great-grandson of an Ethiopian given as a child to Peter the Great, Pushkin is Russia's foremost poet and the creator of its modern literary language. His tempestuous free spirit led to the duel over his young wife in which he was killed when he was thirty-seven-years old. His great literary legacy continues to influence and inspire Russians, who know many of his most famous poems by heart.

house in Moscow in 1826, he wrote a poem for Mariya Trubetskaya, saying goodbye to her friends before leaving on the long route to Siberia to join her husband, Prince Sergey Trubetskoy. It has become a symbol of freedom to Russians, providing comfort in Soviet as well as tsarist times. Its last verse reads:

> Heavy fetters will fall away,
> The prisons collapse—and freedom
> Will welcome you gladly at the entrance
> And brothers will give you back your sword.
>
> (translation by Geoffrey Murrell)

It was not until thirty years later when Alexander II took the throne that the surviving prisoners were released and allowed to return to European Russia.

Orthodoxy, Autocracy, Nationality

Nicholas I ruled for three decades (1825–55). He was a harsh, reactionary man and lacked the charm and humanity of his brother, Alexander. He was called *Nikolay Palkin* (Nicholas the Stick) for the severity and frequency of floggings in his reign, many of them fatal, although to his favor he abolished knouting in 1845, which was a particularly vicious form of beating with a whip of several strands. He seemed to feel more at home in Moscow than in St. Petersburg and would visit the city for long periods of time. He liked to stay in the charming Maly Nikolaevsky Palace in the Kremlin, which was later demolished. He also commissioned the handsome palace, named for his wife, Alexandra, at Neskuchnoe a little south of the Sadovoe Ring. It was constructed in 1826–42 in the late Empire style by Yevgraf Tyurin. In Soviet times it was the headquarters of the Academy of Sciences.

The phrase "orthodoxy, autocracy, and nationality," was coined by the minister for education, Sergey Uvarov, and it became the byword of the reign of Nicholas I. Ironically, it provoked furious debate among the growing number of radical intellectuals in the two cities in the 1830s and 1840s about the history and destiny of the Russian state. Influenced by German and French thought, writers, critics, and students exchanged their ideas in the literary salons of the day, especially in the comparatively free atmosphere of Moscow, far from the imperial presence in St. Petersburg. One school consisted of so-called Slavophiles, mostly based in Moscow—those seeking inspiration for their country from the idealized pre-Petrine past. A second group, opposing the Slavophiles, styled themselves Westernizers; they were more interested in modernity. They accepted Peter's reforms and admired the achievements of western Europe. These movements were not as radically different as their names suggest; both tended to idealize Russia, were opposed to autocracy, and were deeply concerned about the peasant problem.

Nicholas's reign was beset with various revolts against the existing authority, to which he reacted severely and without sympathy, including riots caused by the severe cholera epidemic of 1830–31 in Moscow. Deeply alarmed by the widespread European revolutions of 1848, Nicholas responded by tightening up the censorship laws and further restricting political freedoms in Russia. One of the new institutions of his reign was the Third Department, a secret service intent on stifling freedom of thought. Writers were special targets.

Following the sentencing of the Decembrists in 1826 and the coronation, Russia's greatest poet and founder of its literary language, Alexander Pushkin, was received by the tsar in the Kremlin in the Maly Nikolaevsky Palace. At this famous meeting, Nicholas announced that Pushkin was no longer confined to his estate and had freedom to travel, but he, the tsar, would henceforth act as Pushkin's censor. This was not the act of clemency it seemed but a method by which the tsar could keep the rebellious Pushkin under his control. Their uneasy relationship resulted in Pushkin after his marriage becoming a courtier, which he despised, to enable his wife to attend court. It was to lead to the famous duel between Pushkin and her admirer, Baron d'Anthes, in which the poet was killed at the tragically young age of thirty-seven.

One writer to suffer in a particularly cruel way from Nicholas was Fedor Dostoevsky, born and brought up in Moscow where his father was a doctor. In the 1840s Dostoevsky was already a successful novelist and an active member of the socialist Petrashevsky Circle. When the circle was banned, he and other participants were arrested and subjected to a cruel joke that originated with the tsar. The prisoners were sentenced to death, dressed in shrouds, taken out to be executed, and the soldiers ordered to take aim. When it seemed their last moment had come, the order was suddenly abrogated, the soldiers dropped their arms, and it was announced that the benevolent tsar had commuted the sentence to Siberian exile. The effects of this sadistic joke were to disturb Dostoevsky all his life.

In spite of increasing repression (or perhaps in part inspired by it), the nineteenth century saw the flowering of great literature in Russia, which was largely confined to the two main cities. Because of its many outstanding poets, including Alexander Pushkin, the early 1800s became known as the Golden Age of Russian poetry. Pushkin's novel in verse, *Yevgeny Onegin*, was unsurpassed for its subtle irony, its peculiarly Russian realism, and its simple story vividly expressed. Its effect on subsequent writers was huge. The restless Pushkin liked to pay long visits to Moscow. His fondness for the city is evident from his description of it in chapter 7 of *Yevgeny Onegin* (translation by Geoffrey Murrell):

> Moscow . . . how much is mingled
> In this sound, for Russian hearts!
> How much echoes there!

The poet Mikhail Lermontov, who lived near Moscow in childhood and attended school there, was only slightly younger than Pushkin and, like him, fated to die tragically in a duel. He was the author of fine romantic verse and the classic and subtly ironic novel, *Hero of Our Time*.

If Pushkin can be said to have laid the foundations for the literary language, then Nikolay Gogol, with his fantastic imagination and eye for comedy, the great satirist of *Dead Souls* and the play, *Inspector-General*, was the first great novelist. He was followed by Dostoevsky, the brilliant creator of tormented, guilt-ridden heroes. Ivan Turgeniev, who also had a home in Moscow, chronicled the life of the gentry in elegant prose. Toward the end of the century Lev Tolstoy, whose Moscow house still stands, published his sweeping historical novel *War and Peace*, depicting the war with Napoleon, and the novel *Anna Karenina*, which evokes Russian society after the emancipation of the serfs in the late nineteenth century. The short story writer and playwright Anton Chekhov, a resident of Moscow until he moved to his small estate in the Moscow countryside, was adept at describing ordinary provincial life of the end of the century.

Russo-Byzantine Traditions

Nicholas's preference for "orthodoxy, autocracy, and nationality" can be seen in the personal role the tsar played in fostering the rise of the Russo-Byzantine architectural style as the fashion moved away from classical forms. The turbulent history of the monument to honor the 1812 victory over the French exemplifies this new development.

Immediately after the 1812 war, Alexander I announced his intention to build a memorial church in Moscow. In 1815 he chose the design of the artist and mystic Alexander Vitberg, who envisaged a huge church of three enormous tiers. The lower part, in the shape of a coffin, was to be under ground; the second tier, in the form of a Greek cross, was to support a mighty cylinder with a colossal cupola at the summit. Foundations were dug in the Sparrow Hills overlooking the Kremlin, but problems over the design (Vitberg was not an architect) and misappropriations meant the work stalled. When Nicholas came to the throne Vitberg was arrested, tried, and exiled to Vyatka.

Nicholas reactivated the competition for the memorial and chose the project submitted by Konstantin Ton, whose early churches based on traditional Russian motifs so closely reflected the tsar's outlook. Ton's solution was the huge Cathedral of Christ the Savior, its design borrowed from the early cube churches of Muscovy and those of Byzantium and topped with a single cupola. It cost so much it had to be paid for by public subscription and took over forty years, until 1880, to build on a river site west of the Kremlin, where an ancient monastery was demolished to clear the land. The colossal, lugubrious and heavy church, which could hold ten thousand people, vastly dwarfed everything around it, making it a grotesque foil to the graceful churches and palaces of the Kremlin. Ironically, only fifty years after it was finished it was blown up by order of Stalin to make way for the Palace of Soviets, which was intended to be the tallest building in the world. But the projected palace, which never got far above ground, was abandoned, and an open-air swimming pool was put in its place; then in the 1990s, after the fall of the Soviet Union, the cathedral was rebuilt in all its vastness.

Always more at ease in the old capital than in St. Petersburg, Nicholas commissioned a grand new palace from Ton in the long underused Kremlin. The Great Kremlin Palace was constructed in 1838–49 adjacent to the old palaces of the Muscovy tsars and grand princes. Like Bazhenov's attempt a century earlier to rebuild the Kremlin enveloping the old palaces, Ton's design included within the walls the body of the seventeenth-century Terem Palace and the most ancient church in the Kremlin, the Savior in the Wood. Rastrelli's Winter Palace built for Empress Elizabeth in 1758 was destroyed in the process. The tsar's luxuriously appointed personal apartments were on the lower floor (Nicholas died before it was

CATHEDRAL OF CHRIST THE SAVIOR. The huge ungainly church in the Russo-Byzantine style, which even dominates the Kremlin, was built in 1839–80 as the main memorial to the Russian victory in the 1812 war with Napoleon. Nicholas I personally chose the design of Konstantin Ton, his favorite architect. In 1931 the cathedral was blown up to make way for the projected Palace of Soviets, which was meant to rival the Empire State Building but was never completed. In 1994 it was decided to rebuild the cathedral to symbolize the reawakening of the Orthodox Church after decades of Soviet rule.

completed), while the upper floor contained the reception halls named after the Orders of the Russian Empire: St. George, St. Catherine, St. Vladimir, St. Alexander, and St. Andrew.

Enlargement

The ongoing expansion of Russia—it has been estimated that from 1600 to 1900 Russia grew at the rate of fifty square miles a day—continued in the nineteenth century, although not at such a frenetic pace. By the end of the nineteenth century, Russia controlled Poland and Finland, the northern Caucasus, and huge areas of northern and central Asia, as well as Moldavia and Wallachia on the borders of Germany and Austro-Hungary. It was a vast empire, not even exceeded in the next century by that of the Soviet Union.

In 1851 Nicholas inaugurated the first long-distance railway line in Russia, linking Moscow and St. Petersburg. With the expansion of the railways Moscow acquired nine terminal railway stations from which a tight network of track radiated outward in every direction. The Moscow merchants were quick to take advantage of the extra markets offered by the city's position at the center of the country's vast railway system.

Russian conflict with Britain over Afghanistan and its expansion to the west led to the war with Britain, France, and Austria, allies of Turkey, over the Crimean peninsula in 1853–56. (The Crimea, its population then mostly Tatar, lies south of Moscow and juts out into the Black Sea. It was formerly under the Turks until it was annexed by Catherine the Great.)

The spark that lit the conflict was a dispute over the Holy Places in Palestine. The war was terribly costly in lives lost—Russia lost half a million men, mostly to disease. But a positive outcome of the war was the foundation, in Russia as well as Britain, of a nursing service and greatly improved medical arrangements in the field. Nicholas I, whose intransigence was a major cause of the war, died in February 1855, bitterly disappointed over the looming Russian defeat in the Crimea.

Overdue Reforms

Rather contradictorily, the shock to the Russian people of the loss of the Crimean War created a mood favorable to change. Emancipation, so long discussed in Russian circles, of the twenty-five million peasants still tied to their landlords finally became a real possibility.

Alexander II (ruled 1855–81), unlike his authoritarian father, played a major role in overcoming and in some cases overriding the opposition of the landowners to abolish serfdom. In this he was assisted by the increasingly influential and numerous liberal intelligentsia, mostly residing in Moscow, and by some enlightened officials in the Ministry of the Interior. On February 19, 1861, Alexander, still opposed by many of the large landlords, promulgated the decree that emancipated the serfs. The intention was to grant the freed peasants sufficient land to allow them to make a living, but the conflict between landlords such as the influential Count Panin with his twenty thousand serfs (he owned the lovely Marfino estate north of Moscow) and the liberal reformers in government led to a compromise. Under this agreement, the peasants were given miserly portions of land at prices they could ill afford, which led to long-term debt and great dissatisfaction on the part of both peasant and landlord.

A logical sequel to the great act of emancipation was reform of local government. Hitherto the local squire, acting in the name of the tsar, had administered rural districts, but after the peasants were freed, his authority was no longer adequate, and it became necessary to devise a system of local councils, the *zemstvo*. In 1864 the statute was promulgated by the tsar, who again played the major role: it was he who determined that the new local councils should manage their own affairs with an elected, representative element from both the peasantry and the nobility. By 1880 zemstvo councils had been set up in the Moscow province in Russia's heartland. They were overseen by governors appointed by the tsar to keep them from getting too far out of line. The areas in which the zemstvo made the strongest contribution were those of education and health. They opened much needed schools and hospitals in heavily deprived rural areas.

Local councils were also set up in urban centers, which, although better served by hospitals and schools than the provinces, had been notoriously corrupt and inefficient. Since the reign of Peter the Great, Moscow had been ruled by governors-general, appointed by the emperors and empresses and responsible directly to them. Military governors responsible not only for Moscow but the Moscow province worked under the governors. The governors survived right up to the revolution, but their duties became more formal in 1873 when the new local council (*gorodskaya duma*), elected on a very narrow franchise, and its executive board (*uprava*) came into force. The duma's 160 to 180 members headed by the mayor (*golova*) were elected on a narrow property-based franchise, which in 1889 was only 2.7 percent of the population and which by 1912 had shrunk to 0.5 percent.

Although so few Muscovites had any say in their government, the duma and the uprava carried out impressive improvements in education, including schools for women, medicine, paving of roads (in inner Moscow), and new bridges. They also ran the Belgian-owned electric streetcars and greatly expanded the piped water system by opening a second aqueduct at Mytishchi, although the poorer tenements and small wooden houses (*izba*) outside the Sadovoe Ring remained unconnected. Moscow's poor began to be cared for in a systematic way through a partnership between the city and the rich merchants: lodging houses for the homeless, almshouses, shelters for juvenile delinquents, eighteen hospitals, eleven maternity homes, and ten libraries and reading rooms. There were also nine people's homes (*narodnyi dom*), which provided theaters, reading rooms, and lecture halls. Nevertheless, the great increase in population in the booming city, overwhelmed by the influx from the countryside after the emancipation of the peasants, meant these benefits did not reach the majority of the poor housed in tenements beyond the Sadovoe ring. In spite of attempts at improvement, the city sewage system remained woefully inadequate.

Another of Alexander II's reforms was the system of justice. In November 1864 the tsar introduced new courts, independent of the state, to operate under judges appointed for life, where cases were to be heard in the open before a jury and which could be reported in the press. The former system of administrative law was scrapped, although political cases were still heard before special tribunals and disputes between peasants continued to be settled according to their unwritten, traditional laws.

Nevertheless, the new system was eagerly embraced, thereby encouraging the rise of Russian lawyers, many of whom were in the forefront of social change. One spectacular example of the independence of such courts was a case in 1885. Strike leaders of the large Morozov textile mills fifty miles east of Moscow were arrested for protesting low wages and poor conditions. The jury declared the strikers to be innocent, to the astonishment of Timofei Morozov, the mill owner, who was chastised by the judge for his role in the affair and obliged to pay a huge fine. This case was to act as a beacon for the whole labor movement.

Alexander's reforms did not satisfy many—inevitably, the conservatives thought they went too far, while many of the liberals felt they did not go far enough. Ironically, the very freedoms Alexander had granted, particularly the independence of the universities and the press, led to radical opposition, including the formation of extreme left-wing groups that operated in both Moscow and St. Petersburg and which constantly made attempts on his life.

The adherents of the populist movement that arose in the 1860s and 1870s had believed in achieving a just society in Russia via a peasant revolution or the seizure of power by a revolutionary minority on behalf of the peasants. Radical offspring of the Slavophiles, they believed Russia could follow its own unique path, bypassing Western capitalism. Their early adherents had formed the underground Land and Freedom organization, which had little success. A later offshoot, the People's Will, concentrated on the assassination of government representatives. On March 1, 1881, in St. Petersburg, followers of the People's Will threw a bomb at the tsar's carriage and succeeded at last in causing his death. Alexander's last reform had been to approve a representative national assembly, but he was assassinated before it could be publicized. The decree, if it had been promulgated, might have altered the subsequent history of Russia.

Alexander was followed by Alexander III (ruled 1881–94), a huge man with highly conservative views made understandably more so by the manner of his father's death. Although the new tsar did not completely overturn the reforms of the previous reign, he reduced their impact and called a halt to reforms. One of Alexander's first acts was to hang in public the five members of the People's Will responsible for the assassination of his father, ignoring protests of such eminent figures as Lev Tolstoy.

Alexander's reign was relatively peaceful but proved to be the quiet before the storm. He was succeeded at his death in 1894 by his ill-fated son, Nicholas II.

Moscow's Industrial Revolution

By the end of the nineteenth century, Moscow was sharing in Russia's remarkable progress in science and engineering and enjoying unprecedented industrial growth. The emancipation of the serfs—twenty-two million were freed—helped create the conditions needed for industrial growth, which, in the Moscow area, was predominantly in the production of textiles. By the 1880s the energetic entrepreneur/merchant class was well placed to supplant the declining gentry as the citizens with the most power, wealth, and prestige.

Many of the great merchant families, a large number of whom were Old Believers imbued with a strong work ethic, had owned small enterprises at the beginning of the century or just after the 1812 war. These workshops, where the workers slept on tables next to the machinery or in distressing tenements, were situated on the peripheries of the old city beyond the Sadovoe Ring, in the Zamoskvoreche area across the Moscow River from the Kremlin, or in the countryside circling Moscow, especially to the east along the railway lines near the Vladimir (Nizhny–Novgorod) Road.

The Morozovs were one such family who acquired their wealth in this way. The founder, Savva Morozov, began making ribbons in the village of Orekhovo and selling them in Moscow after the 1812 fire. A serf, he managed over many years to purchase (for a high price) from his landlord, the freedom of himself, his wife, and his five sons. Business prospered, he turned to woolen and then cotton cloth, and at his death left his four surviving sons four textile empires in different towns of the Moscow province. His hugely wealthy grandson, Savva Morozov, was a generous patron of Stanislavsky's Moscow Art Theater and even supported Lenin's newspaper, *Iskra* (the Spark). Like many other merchants keen to disassociate themselves from the classical style of the gentry, he was an enthusiastic patron of the innovative art nouveau style, which strove to break with the artistic movements of the past.

The rapid growth of industry stimulated science and technology in all fields. One of the most interesting was the new science of aerodynamics. The pioneer, Nikolay Zhukovsky,

MOSCOW ART THEATER INTERIOR. Savva Morozov, owner of the huge cotton mill at Orekhovo east of Moscow, and opposite in character from his ruthless father, was a generous supporter of the arts. In 1904 he sponsored the rebuilding of Stanislavsky's innovative theater by the art nouveau architect, Fedor Shekhtel.

built one of the first wind tunnels in the world at Moscow University in 1902. Supported by Dmitry Ryabushinsky, son of the leading banker Pavel Ryabushinsky, he founded the Institute of Aerodynamics at the Ryabushinsky estate at Kuchino, a little south of Moscow. The first airplane in Moscow was built in 1909 at a former bicycle factory near the Peter Travel Palace, where a small airport was opened. Railways were a great impetus to this industrial growth. The most ambitious line, the Trans-Siberian from Moscow to the Pacific, was built from 1891 to 1915 and at 5,811 miles was the longest in the world. By 1914 Russia had become the fifth largest industrial power in the world.

The Silver Age

The growing freedom of expression in the reign of Alexander II was the catalyst in an explosion of creative activity in all the arts known as the Silver Age (to distinguish it from the Golden Age of a century earlier) that began in the last decades of the nineteenth century and continued right up to the early 1920s. It was encouraged by an astonishing number of the new affluent merchant/entrepreneurs like the Morozovs, who, for the most part, were based in Moscow and vied with one another in furthering the latest movements in the arts.

One of most remarkable was Savva Mamontov, a wealthy railway tycoon and amateur sculptor, who befriended young artists, singers, and dramatists like Konstantin Stanislavsky at Abramtsevo, his country home north of the city, where they combined their talents to produce operas and plays, as well as paintings and ceramics. The most famous of all the well-known artists working at Abramtsevo, which included Repin, Polenov, Serov, and Vasnetsov, was Mikhail Vrubel, whose work was to deeply influence the gifted Russian avant-garde artists of the early twentieth century. The Abramtsevo community even turned its hand to architecture and in 1881 produced a seminal building, the beautiful Church of the Savior Untouched by Hand (*Spasa Nerukotvornovo*). It is the first example of the reworking of traditional forms in an exciting and entirely original way and was the model for the art nouveau style in Russia.

In architecture, "art nouveau" indicates the free arrangement of space and use of new materials, combined with unusual ornamentation, in particular the use of wavy lines and natural forms. It was adopted with enthusiasm in Moscow, as well as the rest of Europe, in the 1890s and early 1900s. The most talented architect working in this field was Fedor Shekhtel, who has left over fifty buildings in the city with his indelible stamp. His most spectacular design was the mansion for Stepan Ryabushinsky, with its flat projecting roof, mosaic frieze of dying irises, varied windows in bentwood frames, amazingly fluid staircase reflecting the motif of a watery underground, and the astonishing, secret, Old Believer chapel (Old Believers were then forbidden from building churches or chapels). Other fine architects worked in art nouveau, and Moscow has a plethora of apartment houses, offices, and spectacular private mansions erected in this refreshing and dramatic style.

It was not only in architecture that Russians excelled at the turn of the century. The superb composer, Tchaikovsky, who lived in a modest house in Klin in the Moscow Province on the railway line linking Moscow and St. Petersburg, epito-

BENCH AT ABRAMTSEVO. Savva Mamontov's summer house at Abramtsevo, northeast of Moscow, attracted many leading artists, including Mikhail Vrubel, who designed this ceramic bench for the estate. Vrubel deeply influenced the rising artists of the Russian avant-garde like Malevich and Kandinsky.

RYABUSHINSKY HOUSE. Built in 1901 by Fedor Shekhtel for the wealthy merchant Stepan Ryabushinsky, this house is one of Moscow's most dramatic and successful buildings in the art nouveau style. Maxim Gorky, the writer, lived here when he returned from exile in 1931.

mized the high point of romanticism in music. Tchaikovsky was followed by more innovative composers, including the talented Alexander Scriabin, who invented his own musical language. Scriabin lived in a small house in central Moscow, which is now a charming museum to the composer.

The equivalent movement in the field of literature, symbolism, also arose in Moscow and was expressed through the revival of the popularity of poetry following the long domination of the great novelists. The main exponents of symbolist poetry were Konstantin Balmont, Valery Bryusov, and Andrey Bely, but the most influential was Alexander Blok, who in 1917 was to warmly embrace the revolution.

The title of "symbolism" was also adopted by artists in the Blue Rose group, whose exhibitions were held in Moscow, a more liberal venue than fusty St. Petersburg. The Blue Rose Group inspired by Victor Borisov–Musatov, whose dreamy landscapes are set in a mystical past, attracted many painters, including Pavel Kuznetsov, whose imagination was fed by the lonely steppes of his native Saratov. By 1910 the various artistic tendencies had fused into an avant-garde movement featuring abstraction or cubo-futurism, which was dominated by the art of Mikhail Larionov, Kazimir Malevich, Marc Chagall, and Vasily Kandinsky, along with brilliant women artists: Lyubov Popova, Varvara Stepanova, and Natalya Goncharova. Their exciting exhibitions—like the Donkey's Tail—were held in Moscow and attracted much controversy. These artists continued to display their brilliant talents until the early 1920s when their individual and abstract approach became less acceptable to the new regime, and many emigrated.

At the beginning of the twentieth century, with its population well over a million, Moscow was reveling in these new artistic movements and the wealth accruing to it as the center of manufacturing. The nouveaux riches merchants tried to outdo one another in the splendor of the large new mansions that were sprouting up all over the city. Five- and six-story comfortable apartment buildings also appeared in great numbers, many with large, seven-room apartments, including servants' rooms for the well-off bourgeoisie. The styles borrowed indiscriminately from the past and ranged from pseudo-Russian to a delightfully florid baroque to the drama of art nouveau. There was a spate of new museums, including the History Museum on Red Square, with its pinnacles and forms obviously borrowed from the Kremlin. Red Square was also enlivened with the new Upper Trading Rows, later renamed GUM, on the site of the old marketplace. The large department store of over one thousand shops was divided into three long galleries with three tiers of shops on either side and was cleverly lit from above by arched metal and glass skylights, each forty-eight feet in width.

Concert halls and theaters were built, along with many new motion picture houses (sixty-seven by the time of the revolution). Art galleries included the fine Alexander III Museum (now the Pushkin Museum), the Rumyantsev Museum, and the Tretyakov Gallery (for Russian art). New schools included progressive establishments like Shatsky's Settlement School, which espoused education through the natural development of the child. In line with the rapid increase in literacy, publishing and newspaper houses became part of the cityscape, and many new office buildings and financial institutions appeared, along with a few brave attempts at subsidized housing for the less well off. Moscow, in the early 1900s an enormous and frenzied building site, greeted the new century with confident anticipation.

GUM. The famous department store in Red Square was completed in 1893. It sits in the traditional marketplace, is divided into three long lines and three stories, and is brilliantly lit from above by arched glass roofs set into a metal framework. It was designed like a modern shopping center with over one thousand small shops, a function it still fulfils.

PUSHKIN MUSEUM. Completed in 1912 as the Alexander III gallery of sculpture and art, this building is in the neoclassical style favored in Moscow as the government became more oppressive. The museum was greatly enriched after the revolution by the confiscation of paintings in private hands, especially those of two prescient merchants, Shchukin and Morozov, whose collections of impressionists and early cubist art were unsurpassed.

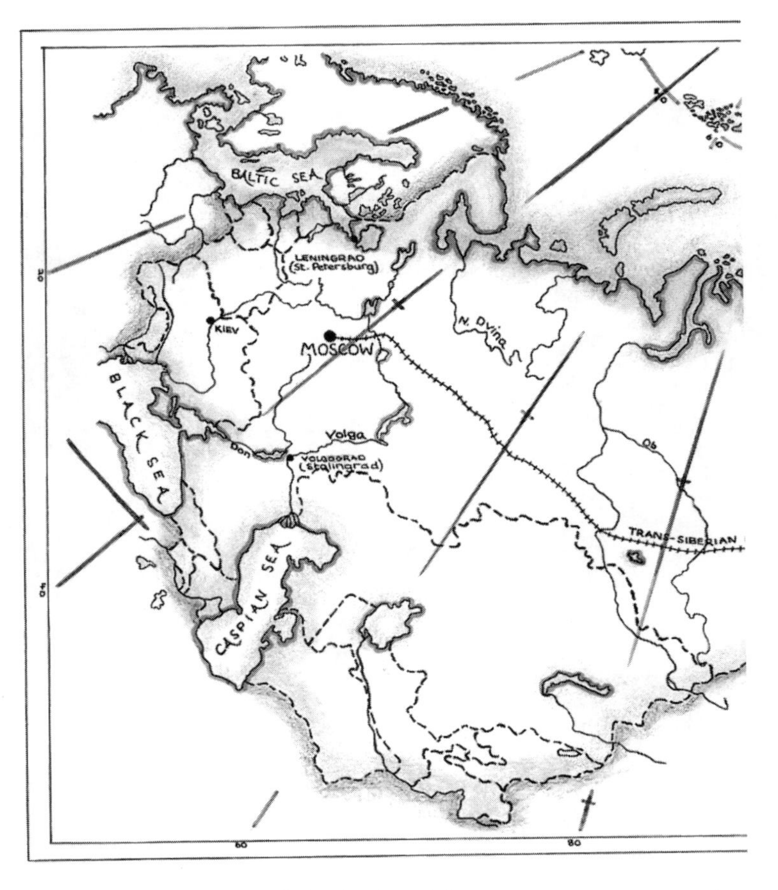

Russia Before 1917 and the Soviet Union. (CREDIT: PAMELA GOODWIN)

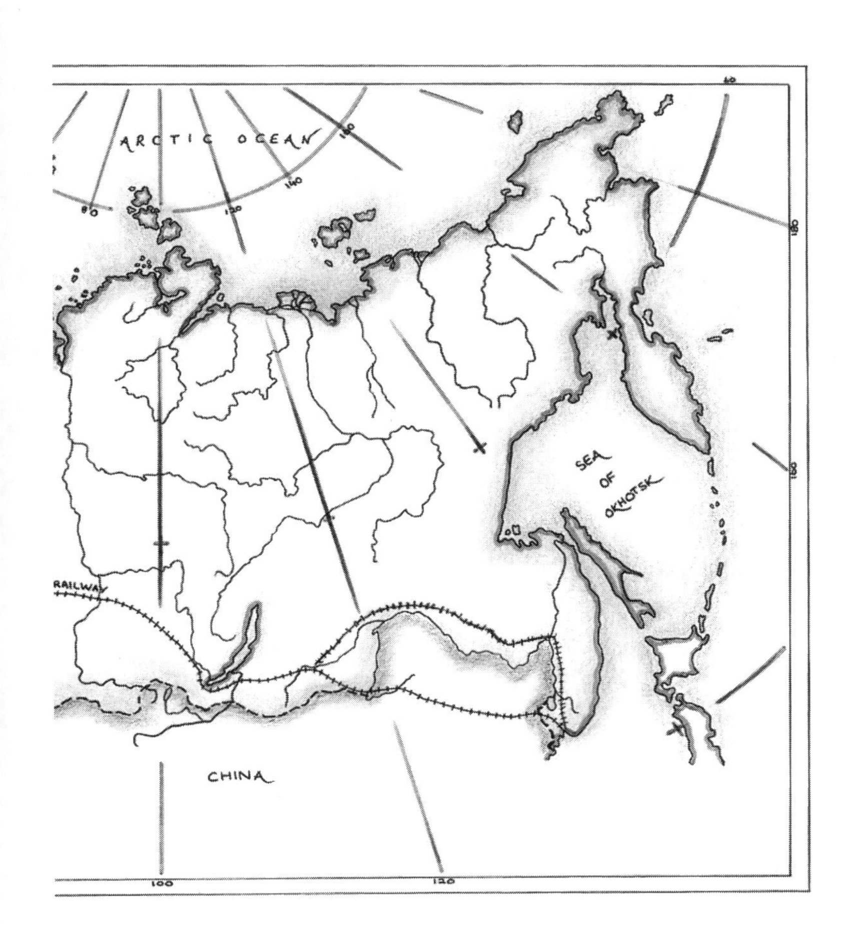

ARCTIC OCEAN
SEA OF OKHOTSK
RAILWAY
CHINA
80
100
120
140
160
180
100
120

CHAPTER 6

REVOLUTIONS AND WARS

Grievances

If Moscow's earlier centuries had been turbulent, the twentieth century was even more disordered. It has already been noted that in the 1880s, after the death of Alexander II, ultraconservative forces once again dominated the Russian political scene. Censorship was reintroduced, close control was imposed over university students, the zemstvo local governments became more cautious, and the national minorities of the empire began to chafe at increasing discrimination against their customs and way of life. Distrust of the lower classes was so great that in 1887 school directors were ordered to reject applicants from the working and servant classes. Opposition to the government from the increasingly literate working classes, the more confident national minorities, and the liberal middle classes began to make itself felt.

Although the power of the nobility began to decline slowly, as the business or merchant class combined with the increasingly numerous middle class rose, there was still a huge chasm between these classes and the great majority of peasants and workers. By the reign of Alexander III's timid

NICHOLAS II AND FAMILY. Nicholas II (ruled 1894–1917), a good family man, was a weak ruler who moved increasingly to the right, constantly changing his advisers. Public disillusionment with the monarchy was exacerbated by the reliance of Tsaritsa Alexandra on the corrupt holy man, Rasputin, for his ability to control the hemophilic hemorrhages of her son and heir. The tsar and his entire family were murdered by the Bolsheviks in 1918.

son, Nicholas II, extremist political groups, particularly of the left, were well established, and the Russian liberal intelligentsia were on the way to becoming dissenters.

In this increasingly difficult situation, Nicholas II, who had succeeded to the throne in 1894, was both weak and conservative, unable by nature to display strong leadership. An ominous start to Nicholas's reign was the tragedy at Khodynka Field in Moscow; as coronation gifts were being distributed a huge crowd surged forward and tripped over army trenches. Some thirteen hundred people were crushed to death. Nicholas openly showed his suspicion of the zemstvo movement, did nothing to prevent anti-Semitic atrocities, and treated other nationalities tactlessly. Old Believers, well represented among Moscow's merchants, continued to be harassed and were forbidden to build their churches. The six million Jews (Russia had the second largest population of Jews in the world), most of whom lived in the Pale of Settlement in the western, formerly Polish, territories, were subjected to pogroms and rioting. Under Nicholas II, many restrictions were imposed on educated Jews, although some still managed to play a prominent part in the cultural life of Russia.

As Russia industrialized, new radical groups formed, which looked more to the growing working class and Western socialist ideology, especially Marxism. Their leaders included Georgy Plekhanov and the law student Vladimir Ulyanov, who later took the name Lenin. In 1898 the Russian Social Democratic Labor Party (RSDLP) was founded, which united several of these groups, including Marxists and trade unionists. In 1903 the RSDLP split into the Bolsheviks (*bolshinstvo*, or majority, which they held only temporarily), the more extreme group under Lenin, and the less radical Mensheviks (*menshinstvo*, or minority), who advocated alliance with the liberals and a democratic constitution. Although from time to time these groups were reunited, the rupture was never properly healed.

The two main cities, Moscow and St. Petersburg, grew at an unprecedented rate—Moscow's population grew from 350,000 inhabitants in the 1840s to over two million by the time of the 1917 revolution—which led to overcrowding and poverty and generated growing discontent among the expanding labor force. The new city governments, although they managed to carry out important improvements, were overwhelmed by the problems of housing, sanitation, education, transport, and health endemic in the rapidly expanding cities. Added to this were periodic economic slowdowns when workers either were laid off or had their already low wages reduced. The severe famine of 1891–92 was another important factor in the growth of militant workers' movements.

Meanwhile the Trans-Siberian railway had opened up the possibility of Russian expansion to the east. A weak China gave Russia concessions in Manchuria and the right to build a naval base at Port Arthur. Japan, also interested in Chinese territory, clashed with Russia, especially after the "Boxer" uprising in China in 1900, when Russian troops entered Manchuria. Although the war could have been avoided if Russia had been more diplomatic, the tsar seemed intent on proving Russian superiority, and in February 1904 the Japanese launched an attack on Port Arthur. By December the Japanese had taken the naval port with huge Russian losses. In May 1905 the Russian Baltic fleet, which had sailed halfway around the world to engage the Japanese, was defeated and sunk in Tsushima Strait before it even reached

Port Arthur. The humiliating defeat led to further disillusionment with the tsar's government.

The Revolution of 1905

The so-called First Revolution was precipitated on Sunday, January 9, 1905, in St. Petersburg by the march of one hundred thousand workingmen, some with their wives, bearing icons and carrying a petition to the tsar. Led by the charismatic Father Gapon, they politely asked for justice and the tsar's protection, an eight-hour working day, as well as freedom of speech, the press, association, and worship. This peaceful but huge manifestation of industrial grievance was met at the Winter Palace, where the tsar was not even in residence, by lines of nervous soldiers. Suddenly the soldiers fired, sending a hail of bullets into the crowd and killing over two hundred demonstrators. A wave of shock and indignation spread over Russia.

While Nicholas II vacillated, sympathy strikes of fifty thousand workers broke out in Moscow in the factories of the Zamoskvoreche area and around the Sadovoe Ring. Trade unions and working men's councils or *soviets*, which made their first appearance in the textile industry, began to be organized. In Poland and the Baltic provinces the strikes were tinged with nationalist feelings, and violent measures were taken to quell them. There were also many peasant disturbances and attacks of an anti-Semitic nature, especially in Odessa. On June 14 the crew of the Battleship Potemkin in the Black Sea near Odessa mutinied over rotten meat served to the sailors. After killing the commander and other officers, they docked at Odessa by the marble steps (made famous in Eisenstein's film *Potemkin*), where the crowd joined them and became violent, looting and burning. Troops fired indiscriminately into the crowd, and over two thousand people were killed.

The strikers of January went back to work, but in the autumn trouble flared again in Moscow, touched off by strikes of the printers. It soon engulfed the entire country. Railway workers also went on strike, and Moscow University students threw open their buildings to public debate over the constitutional problems. By mid-October many factories ceased work, and the movement had taken on the aspect of a general strike.

Sergey Witte, prime minister from 1903 to 1906, demanded that the tsar see reason and establish a constitution. On October 17 Nicholas gave in and published the October Manifesto, granting civil liberties, a wider franchise, and a parliament, the state Duma, which would have the power to pass or to monitor all laws. The unrest continued, but freedom of the press was at last achieved, and in St. Petersburg a soviet of workers' deputies was established with Trotsky, then a Menshevik, at its head. In Moscow, a similar soviet was established in November. But on December 3 the tsar's government took Trotsky and his associates into custody. In Moscow news of these arrests precipitated the strikers to take up arms and occupy the streets. Some thousands of workers, mostly in the Presnya industrial district west of the inner city, manned barricades in the streets or by their factories. The uprising was eventually put down, but only by using extreme force, and in the fray about one thousand people lost their lives. It was a harbinger of the revolution to come a decade later.

Under the force of these events, Nicholas and his government set up the state Duma with members elected by a limited suffrage and an indirect complicated system of voting. (The Senate of Peter the Great was directly under the tsar, and after the 1864 legal reforms it had retained only the function of supreme Court of Appeal.) With all its imperfections, the Duma was Russia's first democratic body, even though the socialists boycotted the first elections, allowing the liberals, the Kadet Party, to dominate. But the nervous Nicholas soon moved to reduce its powers and dissolve the first Duma. The second Duma in 1907 under Pyotr Stolypin was even less powerful. In all there were four Dumas between 1906 and 1917, but Nicholas and his reactionary ministers kept ultimate control over legislation, gradually reducing the powers of the parliament. In this way the opportunity was lost for Russia to acquire a form of constitutional monarchy, which might have saved it from the ensuing revolution and civil war.

Reaction and Neoclassicism

The failure of Russia's first attempt at constitutional government and the consequent triumph of the autocracy of Nicholas II was reflected in the demise of the adventurous and colorful art nouveau period of architecture so brilliantly expressed in Moscow, and the subsequent revival of the classical style. Not only had the monarchy reasserted itself, but also the merchant patrons, who so enthusiastically embraced art nouveau at the beginning of the century, had become the ruling elite and were no longer interested in advertising themselves as different from the establishment. Society as a whole, disturbed by the 1905 events and the failure of the war with Japan, turned in on itself and became more nationalistic.

Leadership by the tsar was not forthcoming, as he buried himself in petty details of government and ignored the profound conflicts and contradictions of the times.

Moscow's new buildings reverted to the safe and secure forms of the late Empire style of the first third of the nineteenth century, the manner in which Moscow had been rebuilt after the fire of Napoleon's invasion. From about 1907 to 1917, charming mansions painted in ochre and decorated with moldings, bays, porches, and Ionic columns began to appear all over the city for this less daring generation of merchants, especially within the Sadovoe Ring. Apartment buildings, office blocks, the great Pushkin Museum of 1912, and even railway stations were built in the reaffirmed classical style. One of the more extravagant was the 1912 mansion for the Tarasov family, a close copy of Palladio's sixteenth-century Palazzo Thiene in Vicenza.

The Great War

As the threat of war moved ever closer, Russia allied itself with Britain and France in the Triple Entente in opposition to the threat of the Triple Alliance of Germany, Austria, and Italy. On the home front, problems remained unsolved, the government became increasingly reactionary, and industrial unrest resulted in heavy countermeasures such as, in 1912, the brutal massacre of striking miners in the Lena gold fields

SPASO HOUSE. This fine neoclassical villa with rotunda resembles the Empire style of a century earlier. Built in 1914 for Nikolay Vtorov, an important arms manufacturer, it is now the residence of the American ambassador to Russia.

in Siberia. In July 1914 the volatile situation in Europe came to a head, with the assassination in Bosnia of the Austrian Archduke Ferdinand by a Serb nationalist. Austro-Hungary immediately declared war on Serbia. Russia leaped to the defense of fellow Slavs amid a great wave of patriotism and enthusiasm for the war. This precipitated Germany's involvement, and then as Germany marched into Belgium and France, Britain declared war against the Central Powers.

At first, Russian troops fought bravely and were able to win several important victories over Austria. But it soon became apparent that Russia was poorly prepared for war and suffered from an appalling lack of adequate supplies, even of uniforms. After a series of defeats, in 1915 the tsar himself took nominal command of the army, thus identifying his autocracy with future military failure. The Russians, fighting on a huge front that stretched from the Baltic to the Black Sea, were heavily overextended. Plagued by the poor supply system, they suffered heavy casualties and increasing numbers of desertions from the army. Nicholas, advised by Tsaritsa Alexandra not to relinquish any power or make any concessions, remained resistant to liberal proposals and constantly changed his ministers, who enjoyed little or no support from the public.

Slowly the government of the country began to disintegrate. By 1916 shortages of staple foods were causing great hardship, and a large number of workers went out on strike. Public antipathy to the war extended to the royal family, focusing on Alexandra who was a German princess. Obsessed with the problems of her hemophiliac son, Alexis, the heir to the throne, she gave her trust to the charismatic holy man Grigory Rasputin, who seemed to be able to control Alexis's crises. But Rasputin, who continued to hold almost hypnotic power over the empress, was not a genuine priest and his debauched way of life and influence over the monarchy shocked society. When some young princes managed, not without great difficulty, to murder Rasputin in Petrograd (as St. Petersburg was renamed in 1914) in December 1916, there was great rejoicing among aristocratic circles, as well as the population at large.

The Revolutions of 1917

The Great War proved to be the final catalyst for the Russian Revolution. By February 1917 the increasing number of walk-outs in Moscow and Petrograd had turned into a general strike. Attempts to put down the strikers were unsuccessful, particularly as many of the police and army sympathized with them. What would have seemed unthinkable only a short time ago now happened. The tsar, who was in his special train at the front near Mogilev, was called on to abdicate. On March 2, 1917, overwhelmed by the enormity of the problems facing Russia, he reluctantly did so. Having decided not to inflict the monarchy on his underage, sick son, he abdicated in favor of his brother, Grand Duke Michael. But Michael was tsar for only a day, for he too abdicated immediately.

For the first time in its history, Russia had no monarch. A Provisional Government was formed, composed of liberal and moderate socialist Duma deputies and headed at first by the popular Prince Georgy Lvov, a Moscow nobleman who had risen to prominence in the zemstvo movement. The socialist Petrograd soviet of workers' and soldiers' deputies, manned mainly by Mensheviks and Socialist Revolutionaries, came into being one day before the Provisional Government was set up. It operated parallel to the Provisional Government, pursuing its own agenda in the interests of the workers and regarding with suspicion most of the activities of the government. By early March the new government had abolished the system of the tsar's governors, which had so hindered the growth of local government in Moscow as elsewhere.

In July Alexander Kerensky, a left-wing lawyer, succeeded in replacing Lvov. Kerensky's advantage was that he was also a member of the parallel Petrograd soviet that met in the same building, the Tauride Palace, as the government. In Moscow, the soviet of worker's deputies was revived on March 1 in the city Duma, along with a soviet of soldiers' deputies to represent discontent in the army. Soviets also began sprouting in the Moscow countryside, especially in Orekhovo–Zuevo, the great textile town.

One of the first decisions of the Provisional Government was to convene a Constituent Assembly to consider a new constitution. But their fatal mistake was their decision to continue the unpopular war in support of Russia's allies, Britain and France. War-weariness had by now so overwhelmed Russia that the army itself, weakened by desertions and low morale, was extremely reluctant to continue fighting.

These conditions proved ideal for the extreme left-wing Marxist groups, the Mensheviks, Socialist Revolutionaries, and Bolsheviks, who dominated the Petrograd soviet. They took the opportunity to announce their espousal of the policy of immediate peace and revolution. Lenin, the acknowledged leader of the Bolshevik wing of the Social Democrats, had been watching events from his base at Zurich in Switzerland. After the February Revolution he managed to return to Russia with the help of the German government, who expected to benefit from his antiwar policies. They gave him a sealed train in which he managed to cross war-torn Europe and arrive on April 3 at the Finland Station in Petrograd. He was given an enthusiastic welcome and immediately announced an uncompromising program: all power must be given to the soviets, land and banks must be nationalized, soldiers at the front should fraternize with the enemy, and the police and army should be abolished. Quickly he became the undisputed leader of the left-wing groups, attracting to his side even his long-term opponent Leon Trotsky and his adherents.

LENIN. Lenin was a charismatic leader able to sway the crowds, as shown in this photograph of 1919. His close colleague, Trotsky, who played a vital role in winning the civil war, is standing on the right at the foot of the tribunal. Lenin was a realistic politician who, after the failure of the first attempts to put communist theories into practice, understood the necessity of returning, albeit temporarily, to market principles in the New Economic Policy. He died in 1924.

Meanwhile, peasants' grievances found direct expression in the unlawful taking of land, and workers in the factories were demanding improvements, as well as better wages. In Moscow, initial patriotism for the war, expressed in intense anti-German sentiment, subsided as the realities of war impinged on the local population. Major factories were moved to Moscow from Riga, and large army garrisons were stationed in the city, bringing a huge rise in the population just as food became scarce and the rationing system broke down. A further source of discontent was the government's heavy hand; from 1912 onward the tsar's internal police prevented Moscow's elected mayors from taking office.

With the virtual collapse of the army and the police, and the ineffectiveness of the Provisional Government, the country rocked from one crisis to another. Demonstrations organized by the Bolsheviks attracted many thousands. In the "July Days," the Bolsheviks nearly overreached themselves, and some of their members were arrested, including, briefly, Trotsky, but Lenin managed to escape to Finland, where he continued to control events. By September the Bolsheviks had gained a majority in both the Moscow and the Petrograd soviets, and they also won elections to local councils in the Moscow workers' districts. Egged on by Lenin, they began preparations for the coup. Lenin came out of hiding on November 6 (October 24, "old style") and took up headquarters in Petrograd at the Smolny Institute, the elite girls' school. (The Julian Calendar "old style", thirteen days behind the Gregorian Calendar in the twentieth century, remained in force in Russia until 1918 when the universally used Gregorian Calendar was adopted.) On the evening of November 7, the battleship *Aurora*, whose command was sympathetic to the Bolsheviks, fired a blank shell signaling the start of the coup. The Winter Palace, where the Provisional Government was meeting, was easily overwhelmed by Bolshevik forces. The ministers of the Provisional Government were taken prisoner, and the Bolshevik revolution was achieved with practically no loss of life.

Although the revolution was bloodless in Petrograd, in Moscow determined armed opposition to the revolution quickly appeared to confront the revolutionary committee of the Moscow soviet supported by left-wing workers. Forces of the Provisional Government, the Whites, mostly military cadets from the Alexander Military School, took up places in the center of the city around the Kremlin. They confronted Red Guards and hastily armed factory workers from the industrial suburbs of Dorogomilovo and Zamoskvoreche south of the Moskva River. It took seven days, November 7 to 14, and the deaths of about one thousand people before the fighting, which ranged heaviest in the streets circling the Kremlin, was finally resolved in favor of the Bolsheviks. At first the Red Guards occupied the Kremlin, but it was soon retaken by the Whites, reinforced by troops arriving by rail. After several days it finally fell to the Red Guards. Damage was inflicted on the Spassky Tower in Red Square, the Ivan Veliky bell tower and the cupolas of the Assumption Cathedral in the Kremlin, as well as on many other buildings.

In Petrograd Maxim Gorky's newspaper, *Novaya Zhizn* (New Life) reported on November 16 that Anatoly Lunacharsky, the Commissar for Enlightenment in Lenin's new government, had resigned on hearing that the Moscow Kremlin had been damaged in the fighting. A few days later he was persuaded it was not as bad as he thought, and he took back his resignation.

All was not yet decided. The Constituent Assembly prepared by the Provisional Government was due to sit in January 1918. Countrywide elections by secret ballot on a universal franchise were duly held December 8–10, a month after the revolution. To the consternation of the Bolsheviks, the elections resulted in a majority for the Socialist Revolutionaries, followed by the Bolsheviks, the national non-Russian parties, the Mensheviks, and the Constitutional Democrats. The liberal parties that had formed the Provisional Government were barely represented. But at the end of its first and only session in Petrograd in January 1918, the assembly was closed and dispersed by Red Guards on the order of the Bolshevik government. It was a harbinger of things to come.

The Capital Returns to Moscow

Early in 1918 the new Bolshevik government in Petrograd found itself in a dangerously exposed position on the northern flank of Russia, pressed by the anti-Bolshevik forces of Yudenich from Finland and by advancing German troops. As the civil war broke out, it became clear that the Bolsheviks, threatened on two fronts by the German and anti-Bolshevik forces, did not control much more than the two major cities. In light of this, it was decided to transfer the seat of government from the Baltic shores to the safer haven of Moscow.

On March 11 Lenin arrived at the Nikolaev (Leningrad) station in Moscow with his wife, Krupskaya, and took a suite of two rooms at the excellent National Hotel, conveniently across from the Kremlin. The day after his arrival Lenin took a walk around the Kremlin in the wet and dirty slush of the melting snow of early spring. He decided that the new government's offices should be centered in the ancient buildings of the Kremlin, the seat of power of medieval Rus. The move from Petrograd/St. Petersburg, the Window to the West that had been created by Peter the Great, to the traditionalist, conservative city of Moscow, still associated with shadowy Byzantine intrigues, was perhaps a foretaste of the darkness and secrecy, the cunning and unpredictable rule of the Stalinist future. Thus, after two centuries, the old capital again took up its role as the center of political power, but the glittering tsars were replaced by dully clad republicans proclaiming to represent the best interests of the workers.

Once more the Kremlin was at the heart of government. It was immediately closed to the public, the monasteries and great cathedrals ceased functioning, and the red banner of the revolution was raised aloft. Many of the Bolsheviks were assigned apartments within the Kremlin in quarters formerly used by the court. Lenin took a small apartment in the Senate building near to his offices (now on show at the estate of Leninskie Gorky south of Moscow). Stalin and his wife lived in the former Poteshny Palace along the west wall of the Kremlin overlooking the Alexander Gardens, and the Mikoyans and Voroshilovs lived nearby. Trotsky, who had an apartment outside the Kremlin, commented that it was very strange to report daily to work through the Spassky Gate, while above hovered the double eagle, emblem of the tsars, not taken down until the 1930s.

Meanwhile, although the revolution seemed secure in the two principal cities of Moscow and Petrograd, the situation was not as straightforward in the rest of the immense country.

POTESHNY PALACE, KREMLIN. When the new Bolshevik government transferred the capital back to Moscow in 1918, its leaders were allotted apartments in the Kremlin. Stalin and his family were given accommodation in the seventeenth-century Poteshny Palace, the tsars' theater of amusements.

Civil War

The dissolution of the democratically elected Constituent Assembly was a major factor in the outbreak of civil war. But the Bolsheviks' first act was in March 1918 to agree to the Treaty of Brest–Litovsk in order to bring about peace with Germany, still a serious threat on the western front. Under the humiliating terms of the treaty, negotiated by the Bolsheviks from a position of great weakness, the new state ceded huge areas of Ukraine and the Baltic provinces and agreed to demobilize. (The treaty was abrogated by the Soviet government after Germany's defeat at the hands of the allies in November 1918.) Fighting then broke out against the Bolsheviks in the south among the Don Cossacks; along the Trans-Siberian railway; in the Northern Caucasus where the White leader, Denikin, was at first successful; and along the Volga, led by Admiral Kolchak.

The war shifted back and forth with terrible atrocities committed by both sides until in 1920 Kolchak was captured and executed, the Whites retreated from Sebastopol in the Crimea, and the northern front fell to the Bolsheviks when allied forces departed in 1919. The latter had been supporting the Whites under British leadership, operating from Murmansk. Bolshevik forces were further aided by the defection of many experienced White officers to their side. The Bolshevik Red Army, under the inspired leadership of War Commissar Leon Trotsky, managed to be everywhere at once by brilliant use of the railways. The trains, decorated with propaganda slogans and pictures, also operated as propaganda vehicles propagating the ideas of communism to a still largely illiterate country people. By 1922 most of the non-Russian nationalities had been returned to the orbit of the now Bolshevik state with the exception of Finland, Poland, and the three Baltic states of Estonia, Latvia, and Lithuania, all of which gained their independence. For the first time in many centuries, the Russian (now Bolshevik) state had shrunk in size.

The horrors of war and then civil war were not quite over, for a terrible famine along the Volga caused by drought and the upheavals of the war occurred in 1921 and led to five million deaths.

Bolsheviks in Moscow

In 1918 the large city of Moscow was still dominated by wooden buildings, although the proportion had fallen to just over half the total. Housing had become even more scarce with the increase of population during the war and the arrival of the Bolshevik government. To solve this problem, house owners were obliged to share their apartments with citizens who were suffering the worst sort of housing in damp cellars and unheated shacks. The owners could keep only one or two rooms; the rest were given over to the needy, and the owners were obliged to share their kitchens and bathrooms with these unwelcome guests. In this way, the notorious communal apartments were born. One and a half million people were rehoused, and many factory workers penetrated the Sadovoe Ring, where the best apartment buildings were situated, altering the social order of the city. Later, as Moscow's population fell during the famine and fuel shortages of 1919 and 1920, the housing problem was alleviated, although not for long.

Tsarist monuments in Moscow were demolished in the summer of 1918 by order of Lenin, including, in the Kremlin, the large statue to Alexander II of 1898 facing the Moskva River, by one of the best known sculptors of the day, Alexander Opekushin. The statue of Alexander III by the Cathedral of Christ the Savior and that of the military hero, General Mikhail Skoboleev, on Soviet Square were also removed. Lenin himself took part in dismantling the splendid cross at the Kremlin's Nikolsky Gate, designed by the artist Victor Vasnetsov in memory of the assassination there in 1905 of Grand Duke Sergey Alexandrovich. The memorial obelisk erected in 1913 in the Alexander Gardens in honor of the three-hundred-year reign of the Romanovs was scraped clean of the names of the tsars and inscribed with those of twenty revolutionary thinkers.

War Communism and NEP

At first the new Bolshevik government took a tough and uncompromising stand known as War Communism in introducing radical communist policies such as nationalization of industry and trade, forcing the peasants to make food deliveries, and the bourgeoisie (mostly townspeople) to do labor-intensive projects. War Communism caused much discontent and a few uprisings—a serious one at the island base of Kronstadt. Eventually, in 1921, in the face of the famine and of hostility to communist policies in a country ravaged by civil war, Lenin backed down and introduced the New Economic Policy, or NEP.

The New Economic Policy, a step backward for diehard communists, was always considered a temporary measure to mitigate the hostility of the country to Bolshevik rule and to allow it to recover after the world war and the civil war. In particular, the peasants, who were becoming adamantly anti-Bolshevik, needed to be won over. Under NEP, a modicum of private enterprise was reintroduced, and concessions were made to agriculture, trade, and industry, although the "commanding heights" of finance, foreign trade, and heavy industry remained in state hands. Nevertheless, these measures ushered in a relatively liberal period in the 1920s, which allowed the economy to begin to recover.

In Moscow the "nepmen," private artisans and licensed traders, were particularly successful in distributing and selling goods, especially bakery, meat, and dairy products, as well as textiles and leather goods, and soon the shortages suffered in the first years of the revolution began to decline. The open-air markets became very active, with many people selling family heirlooms or libraries to make a living. The government set up cooperative stores in competition, but they were poorly stocked, and soon the Soviet practice of waiting in line became entrenched in the system. By 1927 production had been restored to 1913 levels in cereals and livestock and in most industrial goods, with the exception of iron and steel.

But the NEP brought in its wake high unemployment—over one million in 1925. Homeless children, *bezprizorniki*, became a major problem on Moscow's streets; in the early 1920s hundreds of thousands of street children were living by scavenging and petty theft. Gradually, they were rounded up and placed in homes located in former monasteries or stately mansions in the Moscow countryside. The model children's home at Bolshevo, northeast of Moscow in the former estate of the chocolate king, Alexander Kraft, was run on liberal lines in an attempt to reintegrate the children into society. It became a model for others, but by the late 1920s the children were subjected to a more rigid regime to provide cheap factory labor.

New Architecture

It is against the background of a respite from the rigors of communism that one of the most interesting periods of twentieth-century architecture developed. Many liberal-minded people, including artists, had welcomed the revolution, seeing it as liberation from a repressive system of a corrupt monarchy. They interpreted the new forces sweeping the country as an invitation to introduce new ideas and experiment. Artists and those working in the theater, sculptors, and architects boldly experimented with avant-garde design under the auspices of the state. Some had evolved their styles before the revolution, like the painter Kazimir Malevich with his first suprematist work, the abstract painting *Black Square*, but now artists of the caliber of Marc Chagall and Vasily Kandinsky were encouraged by the new regime in special workshops to develop their ideas further.

These artists found themselves working together under Lenin's Plan of Monumental Propaganda, proclaimed in April 1918. It called for the creation of theater, propaganda posters, and street decorations for mass education. It also envisaged new outdoor sculptures of fifty revolutionaries and philosophers to be unveiled for the first anniversary of the revolution. But only twelve were ever made, and of these some were intensely disliked by the public, unused to the style influenced by cubism.

In Moscow, the bust of Mikhail Bakunin, the nineteenth-century anarchist, by V. Korolev was so unpopular it remained covered with boards on its plinth on Myasnitskaya Street until the cold winter of 1920 when the wood was stolen for firewood. It survives in the Museum of Architecture. The less daring obelisk to the Soviet constitution, raised on the newly renamed Soviet Square opposite the Moscow Soviet building (the former Governor's Palace), was unveiled by Lenin on November 7, 1918.

Artists courageously embraced the ideas of the machine age and functionalism (the object or building's purpose is paramount) developing a new, revolutionary style under such exceptional artists as Malevich, Stepanova, and Popova. In Moscow, Vladimir Tatlin, the artist and constructor and originator of the term "constructivism" (utilitarian simplicity and respect for materials), who headed the new Department of Fine Art, designed the exciting and influential Monument to the Third International, or Tatlin Tower. Although it never got beyond the stage of the large model erected for the Party's Eighth Congress, it has served as a beacon to modern architecture ever since. Thus, for a brief moment, Soviet art was in the forefront of the modern art movement.

Many exceptional architects also emerged to try their hand at the new buildings being demanded by the socialist regime in Moscow. Outstanding workers' clubs, libraries, shops, factories, and communal apartments were constructed

SOKOL GARDEN SUBURB. The early Soviet planners were attracted by the concept of garden suburbs to alleviate poor workers' housing. This one at Sokol in northern Moscow has spacious wooden houses with water and electricity in a rural setting like a well-appointed village. Today these attractive houses, which are an island among the tower blocks, are much in demand.

MELNIKOV HOUSE. Konstantin Melnikov built five workers' clubs in the 1920s. According to a Party resolution, they were intended to provide "effective centers of mass propaganda and development of the creative talents of the working class." His own home is in the unusual form of two meshed cylinders with pie-shaped rooms and large studios on the upper floors. It has become an icon of the constructivist period and is still lived in by his family.

in these early years all over the city. Even a garden city of small houses at Sokol was built, and it is now among the most desirable housing in the apartment-dominated city. In Red Square a discreet and impressive mausoleum to contain Lenin's body was constructed to the design of the well-established Alexei Shchusev. Among the most original of the new buildings were those by the gifted young architect, Konstantin Melnikov. His cooperative market at Sukhavrevka is a series of beautifully flowing buildings in angled rows. The angular Rusakov Club projects outward in three heavily cantilevered sections containing the seating for the multifunctional auditorium, which could be reduced or expanded as needed. His own home, built in 1929, is one of the hallmarks of the era. The flat-roofed house and studio is composed of two cylinders meshed together and joined by an interlocking spiral staircase, creating interesting wedge-shaped rooms. The front façade is pierced by a huge first-floor studio window; otherwise, lighting is from regular six-sided windows roughly resembling diamonds that can be covered or uncovered at will.

Melnikov's story is typical of the major designers of the era. Feted in the 1920s, his apogee was his inventive Soviet pavilion that even eclipsed Le Corbusier's contribution at the Paris International Exhibition of the Decorative Arts in 1925. However, with the increasingly authoritative rule of Stalin in the early 1930s, Melnikov ceased to get commissions, and his final executed design at that time was a parking garage in Moscow. (Since then only one more of his designs was executed—the interior of the main department store in Saratov in 1949.) At his death in 1974, although embittered, he was still entering competitions and producing ideas. His Moscow buildings—five workers' clubs, bus and car garages, the Sukharevka market, his own house—are much admired today, although the authorities have yet to establish a museum to the country's greatest twentieth-century architect.

By the end of the 1920s, the fledgling Soviet Union had survived the upheavals of revolution and civil war; with NEP, a modicum of prosperity was beginning to return, the literacy program was well under way, the arts were flourishing, and some freedom of speech was tolerated. But this relatively benign situation was to change drastically.

CHAPTER 7

REPRESSION AND RENEWAL

Rise of Stalin

Lenin died in January 1924, having been incapacitated by a brain disease since 1922. This fact was hidden by his colleagues in the Politburo, the chief policy-making body of the Bolsheviks, who continued to rule in his name. Almost immediately, the official idolization of Lenin commenced as Petrograd (St. Petersburg) was renamed Leningrad. His last "testament" (two memoranda to colleagues) was a warning not to trust Joseph Stalin, the old Bolshevik from Georgia, but it was ignored.

Joseph Stalin, whose real name was Djugashvili, derived his pseudonym from the Russian for steel, *stal*, a true description of his tough, inflexible character. Commissar for Nationalities after the revolution (the Soviet Union contained over one hundred different peoples), in 1922 Stalin also took on the then-unimportant post of Secretary-General of the Central Committee, which he made into a key position from which to accumulate power.

LENIN MAUSOLEUM. When Lenin died in 1924, the Bolshevik government, against the wishes of his widow, decided to embalm and preserve the body in a mausoleum. The first hastily erected wooden building was replaced in 1929 by this marble edifice designed by Alexei Shchusev, the most prominent Soviet architect. The mausoleum was intended also as a tribunal where the leaders could stand to view the biannual military parades. Stalin was interred here in 1953 next to Lenin, until he was removed by Khrushchev in 1961.

The wily Stalin, educated at the Tiflis theological seminary, hid Lenin's testament, skillfully directing the interparty struggle that arose after the leader's death. The Kremlin's corridors of power were filled with the secret maneuvering of one group and another, all of whom danced to Stalin's tune in intrigues that rivaled even those of Ivan the Terrible. Stalin first was supported by the Zinoviev–Kamenev faction against the volatile Trotsky under the slogan "socialism in one country first," opposing Trotsky's policy of permanent revolution or global communism, but the struggle was more political than ideological. When Trotsky was ousted and ultimately exiled, Stalin turned full circle, gathering support against Zinoviev and Kamenev and then the "right opposition" of Bukharin and Rykov. In their place he promoted new men, including Molotov, Kaganovich, and Kirov, who remained loyal as they owed their positions to him.

After the exile of Trotsky, Stalin adopted left-wing policies, including in 1928 the introduction of the Five-Year Plans to achieve rapid industrialization of the country. To overcome the backwardness and inefficiency of small agricultural units and in tune with communist ideology, the collectivization of agriculture was launched in 1929. The extremely reluctant peasantry refused to cooperate and in some places resorted to armed uprisings. Five million peasant households, accused of being *kulak* (Russian for "fist," in this case, village usurers or prosperous peasants) were banished from their lands. Grain and livestock deliveries, forcibly requisitioned from the peasants, left insufficient seed for the peasants even to sow their crops. This led in 1932–33 to a terrible famine that especially affected the Ukraine, Russia's breadbasket. In some cases, people resorted to cannibalism.

Control of the Arts

By the early 1930s the Bolshevik Party, now tightly knit under its ruthless and enigmatic leader, held total and inflexible control over the country. The arts did not escape this strait-jacket. In 1932 all cultural workers—whether in the visual arts, music, or literature—were obliged to join new unions set up in each field, and free expression was extremely restricted. The old independent cultural organizations were closed, and Party *apparatchiks* were imposed as directors of the new unions. It was at this time that the imprecise formula "Socialist Realism" entered the Soviet vocabulary, under which the revolutionary past, the Party, and model Soviet citizens were to be eulogized.

Privileges—including fine country dachas, housing, and access to special shops and schools—were doled out to the obedient through the unions, while those who failed to toe the Party line were deprived of work, regardless of their talent. All branches of life were affected. Those who belonged or were suspected of belonging to the former "exploiting classes" suffered humiliation and hardship, and their children were denied entry to secondary and higher education. For instance, the writer Abramov has revealed that, although his family were poor peasants in the 1930s, his father's ownership of a horse, a "means of production," prevented him from being accepted at the local secondary school.

The Great Terror

It was not long before the increasingly paranoid Stalin began looking askance at his closest party comrades, especially after the suicide of his wife, Nadezhda Allilueva, in 1932. Sergey Kirov, First Party Secretary in Leningrad, was a strong supporter of Stalin until the Seventeenth Party Congress was held in the Kremlin in 1934, when evidence of his great popularity in the Party made him the focus of hope of those discontented with Stalin's increasingly autocratic rule. A few months later, in December, he was assassinated in his office in Leningrad, most probably with the connivance of Stalin, who had begun to see him as a rival. Nevertheless, Stalin treated the death of Kirov as a great tragedy, bringing his body ceremoniously to Moscow to be buried in the place of honor by the Kremlin wall.

The murder of Kirov provided Stalin with the excuse for a countrywide wave of terror against "hostile elements" that culminated in the Great Purge of 1937–38. Because of Stalin's paranoia and the atmosphere of suspicion that pervaded every part of the country, millions, including even loyal Stalinists, were denounced for fabricated crimes, including spying for foreign countries. They were arrested and sent to the huge concentration camps set up by the secret police (at this time called the NKVD) in the remote areas of the Soviet Union. Many were simply executed, as the numerous killing fields in and around Moscow testify. Including those who perished in the camps and those who were executed, it is estimated that at least eight million died as a direct result of the purges. It was indeed a reign of terror by an absolute ruler.

BUTOVO MASSACRES. During the purges from 1937 to Stalin's death in 1953, millions died and millions more were sent to concentration camps in remote areas. At least one hundred thousand people were conveyed from Moscow to this field south of the city, where they were then shot. A church and cross have been erected as memorials to the victims.

Demolition of Churches

Life in the city was thoroughly changed by the revolution. Not only had the notoriously crowded communal apartment come into existence, but also, in the late 1920s, the destruction of Moscow's churches and monasteries began; many priests had already been exiled or executed. Ironically, the revolution had coincided with a renaissance of the church.

Although the office of patriarch—the head of the Russian Orthodox Church since 1589—had been abolished by Peter the Great, who in 1721 replaced it with the Holy Synod, it was reinstated two centuries later as a result of the February 1917 revolution. The church council meeting in the Cathedral of Christ the Savior elected Tikhon as the new patriarch, but the timing of his entry into office two days before the Bolshevik revolution could not have been more unfortunate. As a result of the public condemnation in 1922 by Tikhon of the Bolshevik confiscation of church valuables, he was imprisoned for a time in the Lubyanka and died in 1925.

In 1928 the decision was made to demolish major churches, monasteries, and prominent secular buildings in the city—the small St. Evpl on Myasnitskaya had already been destroyed to make way for a building that was never constructed. Ukhtomsky's lively baroque *Krasnaya Vorota*, the Red Gate, on the Sadovoe Ring was dismantled. The great *Iverskaya Vorota* (the main gate into Red Square that housed the chapel with the famous icon before which for centuries those entering the square had genuflected) was likewise pulled down, to make way for the military parades of November 7 and May Day. In the Kremlin, a small church and the ancient Chudov Monastery and Ascension Convent were dismantled in 1929. This was followed by the closing of all the twenty-three monasteries and convents in the city outside the Kremlin and the removal of all their priests.

In the early to mid 1930s many more churches were demolished, as well as the broad sixteenth-century walls of Kitai-gorod, which encircled the city east of the Kremlin to Bely Gorod, and the great Sukharev Tower of Peter the Great's time. A wide variety of uses was found for the remaining churches and monasteries: as homes for juvenile delinquents, prisons, anticlerical and other museums, workshops and printing works, and even premises for circus animals. Moscow lost nearly half its churches in the Soviet period.

Reconstruction of Moscow

Immediately after the revolution, the new Bolshevik leaders addressed themselves to the task of transforming Moscow into an ideal city, a capital fit for the first socialist state. The first plan adopted in 1924 was discredited in the press as too tame, leaving the center as a museum of old buildings and concentrating new building on the outskirts. The architectural theoreticians played with concepts of a city of communal housing, where life would be thoroughly regulated and children brought up in common. One of the most interesting was El Lissitsky's idea of hanging skyscrapers, the Cloudprop project, which he hoped to place at strategic squares on Moscow's Boulevard Ring. All these dreams, including one project by Le Corbusier, were cut short when in May 1930 the Central Committee issued a decree against utopianism in architecture. Henceforth, reconstruction was to be thoroughly practical, forced to fit in with the new Five-Year Plans for rapid industrialization.

In 1935 for a population now over three and a half million, a new town plan was adopted under Lazar Kaganovich, then the Moscow Party chief, succeeded in the same year by the young Nikita Khrushchev. This plan envisaged criss-crossing the old center with large radial roads and the straightening and widening of the cramped main arteries of the city. However, only the main road, Tverskaya Street (renamed Gorky, now named Tverskaya once again), which connects Red Square to the St. Petersburg road, was subjected to this treatment. In the late 1930s and 1940s it was made three times wider with large new buildings on the east side near Red Square and on both sides further north. A few old buildings, which it was decided to retain, were actually moved back on tracks to gain the required width.

The new buildings were constructed in the heavy Soviet style, a ponderous neoclassicism that became the hallmark of Stalin's Russia. Soviet rule (as in Hitler's Germany) adopted the conservative, imperialist architectural forms of Greece and Rome. Columns and huge archways leading into interior courtyards epitomized these new buildings, heavy cubes broken by rows of windows and cumbersome pediments (triangular, low-pitched gables above doors or windows in classical architecture).

But there are some lighter moments among these serious buildings. One such example is the Red Army Building, not completed until 1940, just north of the Sadovoe Ring. Its shape, dictated by the symbol of the Army, the five-pointed Red Star, is completely unrelated to the functions of a theater. The architect, Alabyan, told Frank Lloyd Wright that he had put in all the columns he would ever use for the rest of his life in the design. Another is the lugubrious Moskva Hotel built in 1932–35. Its left and right wings differ because, it is said, Stalin had approved the two versions of this prestigious new hotel not realizing he was being asked to choose one. No one dared go back to him for clarification, so both versions were built.

MOSKVA HOTEL. Completed in 1935, the hotel occupies a central position near Red Square. It was planned in constructivist style in the 1920s, but by the 1930s constructivism, like the avant-garde in all the arts, was no longer acceptable and it was redesigned in the Soviet classical style. The architect, Shchusev, presented Stalin with a plan showing alternative designs for the two wings. But Stalin approved the design as it stood and Shchusev, not daring to point out his mistake, built the hotel with side wings that obviously do not match. Recent proposals to demolish it have been met with resistance.

METRO STATION LUBYANKA (Dzerzhinskaya). The first line of the Moscow underground system opened in 1935. The highly individual stations were intended to be "palaces for the people" to distract them from deficiencies in Soviet life. The striking station entrance on Lubyanka Square resembles two huge mouths ready to swallow up the crowds.

More substantial achievements took place in the field of engineering. The first line of the Moscow Metro running east–west across central Moscow from Sokolniky to Park Kultury was opened in 1935. It was hailed as a great achievement of Soviet engineering, which indeed it was, although much of the technology had been borrowed from capitalist countries. It was built unusually deep to double as an air-raid shelter—Hitler's Germany was already a threat on the international

STALIN AND THE MOSCOW–VOLGA CANAL. By the end of the 1920s Stalin was firmly in power, and by the mid 1930s he had stamped out all opposition. He is closely associated with the eighty-mile-long Moscow–Volga canal, which was built in the 1930s by labor provided by prisoners. Many thousands died in the construction of the canal, which was dug by hand, without the use of machines.

scene. The spacious and palatial halls were finished in expensive materials like marble and were dubbed "palaces for the people." Yet the subdued tones and fanatical cleanliness of the metro and the tense, silently hurrying crowds of the 1930s when the Terror was in full swing made the underground trains a surreal world. Each station was designed with a particular motif—workers, the revolution, Soviet achievements, or the various nationalities that made up the Soviet Union.

Among other engineering accomplishments of this period are the granite embankments along the Moskva River to prevent flooding (a particularly severe flood had devastated the city in 1908), huge reservoirs in the countryside north and west of the city to provide Moscow with an abundance of water, and the broad Moskva–Volga canal that links the capital to the Volga river system. The canal was constructed in the 1930s under extremely cruel conditions utilizing the labor of hundreds of thousands of political prisoners.

Palace of Soviets

The "grandomania" that swept the Soviet Union in the Stalin era is reflected above all in the project for the Palace of Soviets on the river west of the Kremlin. Frank Lloyd Wright, who visited Moscow in 1937 to attend the Union of Architects' first congress, was appalled at the trend toward ever larger and more imposing buildings, especially the palace. But the Palace of Soviets was the natural outcome of the failed plans to build Palaces of Labor and Industry immediately after the revolution in or near Red Square.

The huge Palace of Soviets, a celebration of the first Five-Year Plan, exceeded all previous schemes by its size and height. Intended for meetings of Party Congresses and the Supreme Soviet, it was to have two halls, the larger to accommodate twenty thousand and the smaller eight thousand. Six round tiers encircled by columns resting on a broad platform were to rise high above Moscow, with a 325-foot statue of Lenin on top dwarfing the Kremlin towers. To prepare a suitable site, another remarkably large building, the Cathedral of Christ the Savior, completed only fifty years earlier in commemoration of the 1812 expulsion of the French, and the main Orthodox church in Moscow since the Kremlin cathedrals had been closed, was blown up in December 1931. In 1937 building work began on the Palace of Soviets, but the threat of war in Europe and problems of leakage from the river prevented it from getting beyond the foundation stage.

The old ladies of Moscow whispered behind their hands that the site was cursed. In 1958 a large, open-air swimming pool was opened on the foundations of the abandoned palace. Ironically, one of the first acts of the new Yeltsin government after the fall of the Soviet Union was to approve the reconstruction of the immense cathedral. Meanwhile, the problem of a venue for Party Congresses was solved by Khrushchev, who approved a new building of glass and concrete within the Kremlin; this building was completed in 1961 and doubled as a concert and opera hall.

The Great Patriotic War

Meanwhile, Germany and the other fascist powers were growing ever more powerful. Aware of the impending danger,

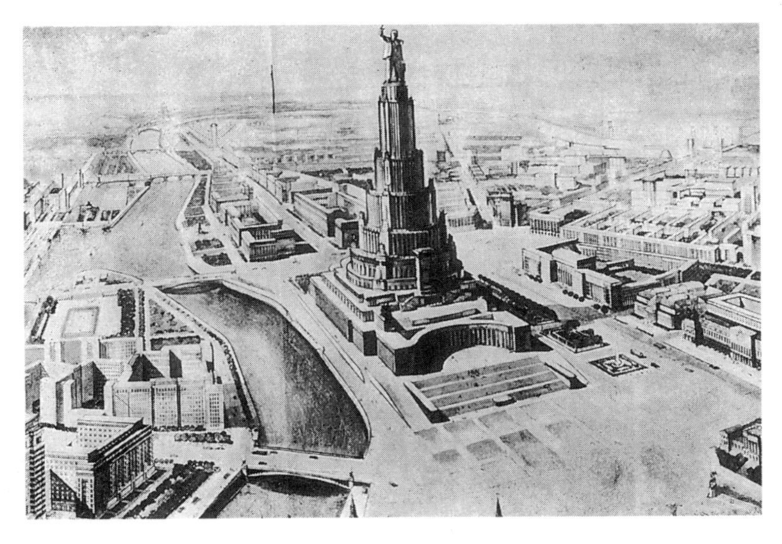

PALACE OF SOVIETS. The tall tower with a statue of Lenin 325 feet high was meant to rival the Empire State Building in New York City. Construction commenced in 1937 on the site of the demolished Christ the Savior Cathedral, but owing to severe engineering problems and the outbreak of World War II, it never got far above ground and was finally abandoned. A swimming pool opened in its place.

the Soviet Union in 1939, on the eve of Germany's invasion of Poland, concluded the Nazi–Soviet Pact, which was signed by the foreign ministers Ribbentrop and Molotov. By this agreement, which included a new partition of Poland, Germany kept its eastern flank safe from the Soviet threat, leaving the Soviet Union free to garner in the independent Baltic states, which were duly invaded in 1940.

The Russian breathing space soon ended, however, when Germany invaded in June 1941. Thus, willy-nilly, the Soviet Union found itself allied to Britain first and then the United States when it entered the war in December 1941. Stalin had refused to heed warnings from Western statesmen about German intentions, and, weakened by purges of the army in the late 1930s, the Soviet Union found itself unable to halt the rapid German blitzkrieg. The Soviet forces retreated, pursuing a scorched-earth policy that was especially hard on the undefended local population. The German army overran the Ukraine. But they made a series of fatal errors. First, their hatred of Slavic peoples prevented them from accepting the welcome given them by many people in the Ukraine and Belorussia, who believed the Germans would save them from Soviet communism. Meanwhile, Stalin craftily began wooing the Orthodox Church, even allowing the reopening of some churches, and he permitted closer contacts with the West and some concessions to freedom of speech. Resistance stiffened against the Germans. Although they subjected the one million inhabitants of Leningrad to a lengthy and sustained siege that lasted three years, they failed to take the city.

Battle for Moscow

By mid-October 1941 the government had panicked, Moscow was evacuated, and valuables—including Lenin's body—were moved to Siberia. Stalin did not leave the Kremlin and move to Kuibyshev (Samara), as foreign embassies and government departments did, however. As Moscow and the Moscow province accounted for 25 percent of the industrial output of the Soviet Union, many factories were also moved eastward to safer regions. If Moscow had fallen into German hands as the Germans expected, it would have been a great victory for Hitler. By November the German army had succeeded in reaching the countryside west, southwest, south, and north of Moscow, including the village and fields of Borodino, where Napoleon had faced the Russians in 1812.

In this bleak moment, Stalin presided over the traditional eve of the anniversary of the revolution ceremonies on November 6, held this year in the safety of the Mayakovskaya metro station. On November 7 he reviewed troops on Red Square as usual, but this time the young soldiers marched off the square to the front to engage the Germans. Near Volokolamsk on November 16, twenty-eight Russian soldiers desperately fought off a German tank attack and managed to destroy fourteen of twenty in the first wave. When the second wave of thirty tanks came at them, they wrapped grenades around themselves and became suicide bombers. Only five Russians survived the battle, but the German advance was held up for four hours, long enough for reinforcements to arrive.

Nevertheless, German scouts were able to infiltrate as far as Khimki on the Leningrad Road, less than twenty miles from the Kremlin. A memorial of crossed railway tracks—like the "hedgehogs" which had been hastily put together to stop the German tanks—stands at this point near the Sheremetevo international airport. But here and elsewhere on Moscow's periphery, their progress was halted in December 1941 when Marshal Zhukov inaugurated the successful counterattack.

The German defeat in the Moscow region was caused not only by fierce Russian resistance but also because of the distance from their supply bases and the severe weather. Unbelievably, trusting in their rapid advance, the Germans were unprepared for the severity of the winter, which was particularly harsh that year. Slowly they were forced back.

About three hundred fifty of Moscow's buildings were damaged by German bombing in the autumn and winter of 1941, including a direct hit on Party headquarters, but these were minor events compared to the destruction of Leningrad during its long siege. There was great personal suffering in Moscow, however. In the extremely severe winter of 1941–42 there was very little heating and electricity for those who remained in the city. The deep metro stations proved effective shelters, and people moved there for the night. About 10 percent of the population of Moscow died during the war, and two-fifths moved to other cities, some returning in 1943 when the tide turned.

In the south, Sevastopol and the Crimea fell in July 1942 to the Germans who again advanced, this time toward the Volga and the Caucasus and the rich oil resources of Baku. To advance, they had to take Stalingrad situated on the southern reaches of the Volga before it reaches the Caspian Sea. The siege of the city began in August 1942, but the determined resistance of the Soviet army meant that the battle lasted until January 1943, when the Soviet army managed to defeat the Germans. In the process they captured the whole of the Sixth Army, including its commander General Paulus. Stalingrad was the most decisive victory for the allies in the entire war. The Soviet army gradually pushed the German army back through the Ukraine, and it swept through eastern Europe, taking Berlin on May 2, 1945.

VICTORY DAY 1945 IN RED SQUARE. In autumn and winter 1941–42, the German army got dangerously close to Moscow before being forced back; in some cases German scouts were only nineteen miles from the city center. At a ceremony to celebrate victory in Red Square in May 1945, Russian soldiers threw down captured German flags.

The realities of the military situation dictated that Eastern Europe—Poland, Czechoslovakia, Hungary, Romania, and Bulgaria—should fall into the Soviet sphere of influence under the agreements of the Big Three (Churchill, Roosevelt, and Stalin) at their historic meetings in Teheran in 1943 and in Yalta and Potsdam in 1945. Vanquished, Germany was divided into four occupation zones by the allies (Britain, France, the Soviet Union, and the United States): northwest to Britain, southwest to France, south to the United States, and east to the Soviet Union. Berlin, which lay within the Soviet zone, was administered by all four.

The Cold War

At the end of the war, it is estimated that the Soviet Union, justly proud of its victory, had lost more than twenty million soldiers and civilians. Soon plans were made to rectify the terrible destruction wrought by the war. Special efforts were expended to rebuild Stalingrad (renamed Volgograd in 1961) and to restore Leningrad and the fabulous royal palaces that surrounded the city, which had been deliberately destroyed by the retreating Germans. Towns and villages west of Moscow had also been devastated by the war. The splendid Resurrection Monastery at Istra, built by Patriarch Nikon in the seventeenth century, had been deliberately fired and mined, its tall bell tower demolished and the vast cupola left in tiny fragments. Plans were made to rebuild even before the war ended, and in 1945 Alexei Shchusev, the leading Soviet architect, set to work. It has taken many decades, but the amazing church, inspired by the Church of the Holy

Sepulchre in Jerusalem, is once again whole. The bell tower was not rebuilt.

By 1948 industrial output had largely recovered. However, the friendly relationship between the victorious allies and the Soviet Union did not long survive the end of the war. Once more, the familiar xenophobia began to be exhibited by Stalin and his henchmen. Stalin proudly and suspiciously refused aid from the United States under the Marshall Plan and forced his East European satellites to do the same, although during the war he had been happy to receive American and allied equipment and food. Soviet soldiers who had survived Hitler's concentration camps were rearrested as they stepped over the border into the Soviet Union, where they were accused of treason and sent directly to Soviet concentration camps. The writer Alexander Solzhenitsyn, who had fought bravely as an artillery officer, was imprisoned in the Gulag because of letters criticizing Stalin that were opened by the censor. By 1949 communist regimes had been established in all the eastern European countries within the Soviet sphere of influence, and Germany had been divided into two states, communist East Germany and democratic West Germany.

Postwar Megalomania

As he grew older (he was seventy in 1949), Stalin's megalomania seemed to have no bounds. It was decided to encircle the old city with eight high-rise buildings emulating American skyscrapers. Seven were built between 1949 and 1957, several over thirty stories high. They resemble tiered wedding cakes embellished with spires, pinnacles, and Soviet stars, the epitome of the Stalin Gothic style. Six were built around or near Moscow's inner Sadovoe Ring, while one, the new university building, was situated in a suburb south of the old center. From a distance they provide the city with vertical uplift and have become familiar landmarks, although maintenance of the elaborate facades is a continuing problem. At the same time, new metro lines were opened—indeed, the authorities boasted that work on the metro never ceased even during the war.

By 1948 not only was the Cold War clearly established but also the slight freedom allowed the arts during hostilities was abruptly withdrawn. Under the Central Committee secretary in charge of ideology, Andrey Zhdanov, leading personalities in literature, like Akhmatova and Zoshchenko, and the musicians Shostakovich and Prokofiev were severely criticized and accused of "formalism." Although they themselves were not arrested (Prokofiev's first wife, Lina, was sent to the camps for eight years), their work ceased to be performed, and their means of livelihood were seriously threatened. It was a signal to those in all the arts that no one was immune from Party control.

As his paranoia grew, Stalin planned renewed purges and the deportation of Jews to Siberia. "Plots" against the regime were fabricated, including the notorious anti-Semitic Doctors' Plot in January 1953, in which it was alleged that nine Jewish doctors intended to murder prominent Soviet figures. But before the trials could be held, Stalin died a natural death on March 5 at his Near Dacha in the suburb of Kuntsevo at the age of seventy-four. Sergey Prokofiev died in Moscow on the same day, but his death was practically unnoticed in the mass hysterical mourning for Stalin. So

HOTEL UKRAINE. Seven "wedding-cake" towers, some over thirty stories high, were built in Moscow in 1949–57; they included the Hotel Ukraine on the Moskva River. In 1954 after Stalin's death, Khrushchev criticized the excessive decoration and expense of pompous Soviet buildings, particularly citing the wedding-cake towers, when new housing should have been the priority.

many came to view Stalin's body laid out in the Hall of Columns of the former Nobles Club that huge crowds built up, filling the back streets all the way to the boulevard. The crush led to a stampede in which many people lost their lives. Stalin was ceremoniously laid to rest in the mausoleum built for Lenin in Red Square, next to the first Bolshevik leader. In the concentration camps there was great rejoicing among the hundreds of thousands of prisoners held in the inhospitable lands of the Soviet north. It was to be two to three years before most were able to return home.

After Stalin's death, some relaxation in Soviet intellectual life occurred almost immediately. In 1954 Ilya Ehrenburg's *The Thaw*, from which the period takes its name, was published, followed in 1956 by Vladimir Dudintsev's *Not by Bread Alone*, which implicitly criticized the inhumanity of the Stalinist system and restored the value of the individual and importance of private life. It was decided to reopen the Kremlin cathedrals and museums, which had been firmly closed to the public since 1918. These were glimmerings of hope after the long nightmare of Stalin's reign.

Khrushchev's Ascendancy

The new government was called a "collective leadership" of Stalin's three most powerful lieutenants: Georgy Malenkov, Nikita Khrushchev, and Lavrenty Beria. The first to fall was the dangerous Beria, the head of the secret police, who was executed secretly only a few months after Stalin's death. At first, Malenkov seemed to be the most important leader, but by the end of 1953 Khrushchev, who had eleven years' experience in the Moscow Party apparatus and who held the key post of First Party Secretary, was clearly in the ascendant. He succeeded in consolidating his position at the Twentieth Party Congress in February 1956, when, with great daring, he denounced the "cult of personality" of Stalin and the executions and terror. Although he limited himself to injustices against members of the Party, the speech, which soon became known in the West and therefore through foreign broadcasts to the whole of the Soviet Union, inspired feelings of relief that the excesses of Stalinism were now over. It did not yet mean the end of the communist regime, although in the same year it inspired uprisings in the beleaguered East European states, especially Poland and Hungary, which were brutally put down in the latter by Soviet troops.

In 1957 Khrushchev's position was cemented when he ousted the "Anti-Party Group," as he called it, which included his former colleague in the Moscow Party organization, Kaganovich. In 1958 Khrushchev replaced Bulganin as head of government, thus assuming leadership in both Party (First Secretary) and government (Chairman of the Council of Ministers). (In theory, and according to the constitution, government bodies at all levels exercised executive authority. In fact, Party organizations, with the Presidium or Politburo at the summit, made all important political decisions.)

Khrushchev made bold if fruitless efforts to tackle the perennial agricultural problem of low yields and insufficient supplies of grain. In years when the crop was poor, the Soviet Union was not able to produce sufficient grain to meet the needs of its people. One of Khrushchev's ideas, the planting of the vast virgin lands of the Kazakh steppe and western Siberia, at first resulted in good harvests then declined as much of the newly cultivated land turned into a dust bowl. He espoused the charlatan biologist, Trofim Lysenko, whose spurious theories promised vastly improved yields. He also impetuously declared that the Soviet Union would achieve full communism, a state of utopia, in twenty years, although it was obvious the problems of even catching up with the West could not be realized in that time. But the Soviet Union was then basking in the achievements of its space scientists, especially when Yury Gagarin, who completed his studies at the Zhukovsky air academy in the old Peter Travel Palace in Moscow, circumnavigated the earth in April 1961 in a space capsule, the world's first manned space flight.

Khrushchev tolerated more freedom in the arts than his predecessors, but he could not help imposing his own limited opinions. In 1962 he suddenly appeared at an exhibition of modern art in the Manege hall near the Kremlin and engaged in acrimonious debate with some of the artists. Significantly, the artists, unlike those of an earlier generation, were not inhibited from expressing their views, even to the Soviet leader. However, Khrushchev's disapproval still meant the exhibition quickly closed, and a general clampdown on the arts ensued. Literature was also becoming more daring, and although Pasternak was denied the right to receive the Nobel Prize in 1958 for *Dr. Zhivago,* which was not even allowed publication in the Soviet Union, Khrushchev personally intervened to allow Alexander Solzhenitsyn to publish in 1962 his epoch-making book *One Day in the Life of Ivan Denisovich,* set in a concentration camp.

During the Twenty-second Party Congress in 1961 when Khrushchev extended the de-Stalinization process, Stalin's body was secretly removed in the middle of the night from the mausoleum where it had lain next to Lenin's and was reburied behind near the Kremlin wall. There could be no more vivid statement of Stalin's demotion in Soviet history.

Khrushchev was a fascinating, highly intelligent if ill-educated and erratic leader, whose tendency to be drawn into dangerous international disputes and to launch extravagant and hare-brained economic schemes made him increasingly suspect in the eyes of his colleagues. Although he made a successful visit to the United States in 1959, the first Soviet leader to do so, only three years later he attempted to put Soviet nuclear missiles into Cuba. The American president, John F. Kennedy, in a famous showdown succeeded in getting Khrushchev to back down. The Soviet elite were embarrassed by Khrushchev's clownish behavior when abroad, such as the occasion when he lost his temper at the United Nations and angrily banged his shoe on his desk. On October 14, 1964, Khrushchev was removed from office by his colleagues in the Central Committee and forced to retire on grounds of "ill health." He was not, as would have happened in the past, subjected to a show trial and executed but was allowed to live out a peaceful old age at his dacha among those of the Soviet elite on the banks of the Moskva River.

Urban Expansion

Khrushchev also stamped his personality on Moscow architecture when in 1954 he criticized the excesses and expense of the Stalin skyscrapers and called for more simplicity and standardization, including prefabrication. His intention was to achieve rapid and inexpensive construction to alleviate the housing problem. The population of Moscow had grown enormously after the war, which, with the paucity of new housing in the Stalin era, meant that apartments in the old center were extremely overcrowded with in some cases ten persons to a room. In an effort to deal with this problem, Khrushchev in the late 1950s approved the rapid construction of five-story apartment buildings (elevators did not need to be installed in buildings of five stories or less) in the new *microrayoni* of the expanded city. The apartment buildings were intended to have a life of only twenty years. Although today these apartments, known as *Khrushchoby* from a combination of Khrushchev and *trushchoby* (slums), appear mean and tiny, in the 1960s with their separate bathrooms and kitchens they seemed luxurious to the average Muscovite living in the cramped communal apartments.

In August 1960 Moscow's boundaries were greatly enlarged, more than doubling its territory (and increasing the population to over six million). A new ring road of sixty-eight miles was built surrounding the expanded city. From the 1960s to the 1980s, vast housing schemes, some of twenty-story tower blocks were hastily and often poorly constructed, as well as poorly maintained, in the new suburbs. The buildings soar above the low central streets of the heart of the city in a protective ring. The majority of Muscovites live in these modern apartments, usually of two rooms with kitchen and bath, but most also have access to summer cottages or *dachas* in the unspoiled countryside around the metropolis.

MODERN TOWER BLOCKS AT TROPAREVO. Under Khrushchev, in 1960 Moscow was greatly enlarged, and a huge program of apartment blocks was inaugurated in the new areas. At first they were five floors without elevators, but in the 1960s to 1980s high-rise towers of twenty stories and more were erected, which greatly relieved the scandalous heavy overcrowding of the old center.

Brezhnev and Stagnation

Khrushchev was succeeded by the second collective leadership in which Leonid Brezhnev—like Stalin as General Secretary—played the leading role. Although the Party still retained tight control, government was less subject to erratic whims as had been the case under Khrushchev, and some of the more irrational agricultural reforms were halted.

However, the de-Stalinization process begun by Khrushchev also declined, so that in the 1970s there was a more positive reappraisal of the role of Stalin. No more literature like Solzhenitsyn's gripping description of camp life was allowed to appear, and some dissident writers were tried and imprisoned. This more conservative approach exemplified Brezhnev, around whom an increasing cult of personality developed and who, like Khrushchev, became head of government as well as chief of the Party (although the Party position was the more important). In spite of Soviet intervention in Czechoslovakia in 1968 to halt the liberal reforms taking place there, relations with the United States and western Europe improved, especially with the visit of President Nixon in 1972 when the SALT 1 agreement limiting nuclear missiles was signed. In the Helsinki Agreement in 1975, the West recognized the postwar frontiers in Europe in return for Soviet concessions on human rights. Relations worsened again when the Soviet Union invaded Afghanistan in 1980 to aid their puppet government there.

In retaliation, the United States and some other countries refused to attend the Olympic Games held in Moscow in 1980. This was a great disappointment for the city as new stadiums, swimming pools, and a special Olympic Village had been built, and there was a general air of anticipation at the honor of holding the games. In the countryside where some of the sports like canoeing and sailing were held, there was an effort to improve roads and tidy up some of the churches that would be seen by the participants and public on their way to the sporting venues.

This period of stagnation (*zastoi*) was, as the name implies, a period of few initiatives. The average age of those serving in the governing body of the Party, the Presidium or Politburo, was over seventy by the 1980s. The Brezhnev era became famous for the corruption and nepotism that prevailed at all levels of government and in the national republics and regions. Some scandals such as those in the caviar industry, cotton production in Uzbekistan, and the illegal sale of icons abroad erupted openly. Those espousing so-called dissident views critical of the regime were hounded, arrested, or, as in the case of Solzhenitsyn in 1974, expelled. But on the whole, people within clearly defined limits lived without the fear that had so marked Stalin's rule. Some dissident views and forbidden literature were disseminated through the system of *samizdat*, or self-publishing, which flourished on a huge scale among the intelligentsia. Solzhenitsyn's monumental denunciation of Stalinist repression, *The Gulag Archipelago*, was copied on typewriters in many homes in Moscow and given to friends, who read it secretly and passed it on. Disillusion with communism was ardently discussed among like-minded friends in the apartments of the intelligentsia but still was not openly expressed.

Perestroika and Glasnost

Leonid Brezhnev died in 1982. He was succeeded by the head of the KGB (the secret police renamed in 1953), Yury Andropov, an intelligent man who was intent on rooting out corruption, but he hardly had time to show his mettle when he, too, died in February 1984. The cautious leaders chose another elderly and ailing politician, Konstantin Chernenko, who was in his seventies. Already ill, he too did not last long and died from emphysema in March 1985.

This time the Politburo, after long argument, boldly chose as their leader the much younger and more energetic Mikhail Gorbachev, aged fifty-four. Gorbachev, with his degree in law from Moscow University, was better educated than most members of the Politburo. He had been impressed on visits to Italy and Canada with the prosperity of those countries and determined to initiate economic reforms in the Soviet Union. One of his first measures was the extremely unpopular edict restricting the sale of alcohol, drink being the principal social problem of the Russians and a major cause of inefficiency in the labor force.

Gorbachev then turned to the economy. He rightly viewed the main impediment to reform as lack of initiative and refusal to accept responsibility, which was inbred in the Soviet system. He determined that if people had more freedom to do as they saw best, instead of obeying directives from on high, they would take pride in their work and would stop the endemic pilfering, dishonesty, and sheer apathy that so affected the system. It was to get the economy moving, therefore, that Gorbachev tentatively began taking the lid off state control.

His initial policies, however, were intended to make the existing system function more efficiently, not change it, and were introduced under the slogan "acceleration" (*uskorenie*). But soon he became convinced that more radical reform was needed and advanced a new slogan, *perestroika* (restructuring), which implied fundamental changes. He also came to realize that serious reform and innovation would not happen without freer discussion and exchange of ideas, and he sponsored the policy of *glasnost*, or greater openness in public life.

At the end of 1985 Gorbachev got rid of Victor Grishin, Moscow's corrupt Party Secretary of the Brezhnev era, appointing in his place the energetic and lively Boris Yeltsin from Siberia, the first Party official to fill this post who was not of the "Moscow clique" (those who made their career in Moscow). Yeltsin immediately set out to show he was a man of the people by tackling the problems of distribution and supply of consumer goods and food. He dismissed his official car and traveled by metro, mingling with the ordinary Muscovites to their astonishment. It was then unprecedented for Party officials to be seen on the streets or in the underground without the protection of their huge black limousines that would cruise down the center of the road in specially demarcated lanes. In his bombastic way, Yeltsin would call unexpectedly at shops or enterprises to assess the situation. He not only tried to clean up city government, but also he slowed the flow of ever more industry to the city (industry was overconcentrated in Moscow and the region) and began the battle against pollution. He even inveighed against ugly architecture. He was instrumental, too, in beginning the process by which Moscow's churches began to be reopened. He personally intervened in the case of the Great Ascension Church at Nikitsky Gate on the Boulevard where Pushkin was married. For decades in use as an electricity substation, Yeltsin promised to turn it over to the local parish. When the enterprise was slow to remove its equipment, he angrily marched into the building and forced their rapid departure. In 1986 he was elected to the Politburo, the policy-making organ of the USSR. But his constant criticism of the leadership and attempts to hasten reform of the Moscow government led in November 1987 to his dismissal and replacement as head of Moscow by the more conservative Lev Zaikov.

At the Twenty-seventh Party Congress in March 1986, nearly half of the Central Committee were new, Gorbachev people, and the average age fell precipitously. But only a month after the Party Congress, a serious explosion occurred at the nuclear reactor at Chernobyl in the Ukraine, the most terrible nuclear explosion in peaceful times. Fallout extended from Turkey to Poland and even western Europe, but ironically not over Moscow. At first, the accident was concealed from the Soviet public, but in the face of evidence from western monitoring devices, five days later it was fully reported.

Ironically, this terrible accident assisted the media in its campaign for open reporting. After Chernobyl, some newspapers like *Moscow News* and the monthly *Novy Mir*, also published in Moscow, began reporting on hitherto forbidden subjects and increased their circulation many times. Books that had been sitting "on the shelf" were allowed to appear, including Anatoly Rybakov's *Children of the Arbat* and novels by Zamyatin and Mandelshtam. Equally important was the film by Tengiz Abuladze, *Repentance*, a gripping depiction of the Terror that left many in the audience in tears. The theater, too, reflected this honest looking back with the eruption of political plays including Mikhail Shatrov's *Dictatorship of Conscience* at the Lencom theater in Moscow involving the blasphemous idea of a mock trial of Lenin.

In the visual arts, the formerly despised avant-garde of the early years of the century were rehabilitated and shown at special exhibitions in the Tretyakov Gallery. Moscow's modern artists, up to then denied membership in the artists union, were tentatively given space in galleries, and Ilya Kabakov, the well-known conceptual artist, spoke out in print against past repressions.

Gorbachev also encouraged a rapprochement with church leaders. The leading but extremely dilapidated monastery in Moscow used to house juvenile delinquents, the Danilov, was given back to the Orthodox Church for the patriarch's use. In 1988 the millennium of the Orthodox Church was celebrated in style. The sound of church bells silenced since the revolution rang out again, a portent of the new era. In the next few years more than a hundred closed churches, no matter their condition, were reopened and repaired.

Collapse of Soviet Power

But Gorbachev's relatively benign attitude to the arts was still under the umbrella of the Communist Party, which he had no intention of dissolving. He fostered elections in which non-Party members were allowed to stand, and the results were not always predictable. As events began to spiral out of his control, the old guard of the Party and particularly the army and the security forces, the KGB, became increasingly uneasy. And the countries of eastern Europe, satellites of the old Soviet system, began agitating for independence.

In 1989 a series of dramatic events made the process unstoppable. After Gorbachev's visit to East Germany in May, hinting at his agreement for free elections, events rapidly progressed, culminating in the fall of the Berlin Wall that divided the two Germanys in November, followed by the collapse of East Germany. The other East European satellites quickly followed suit, grasping their independence; only in Romania where the leader, Nicolae Ceaușescu, refused to step down was the transition bloody.

Within the Soviet Union, the national republics avidly followed these events, especially Azerbaijan and Armenia, the Baltic states, Moldavia, and Ukraine. In these republics national movements grew in importance, galvanized by the incident in Georgia in April 1989 when peaceful demonstrators in Tbilisi were attacked by troops of the Interior Ministry and some were killed. The Lithuanian parliament was the first to declare sovereignty in March 1990, and by the end of the year all the other republics had followed suit, although none actually broke away from the Soviet Union at this stage. In Russia itself, Russian interests were being promoted by Boris Yeltsin, who was by now a threat to Gorbachev's authority. In the June 1991 elections, Yeltsin, who had resigned in 1990 from the Party, was elected president of the Russian Republic (Russian Soviet Federative Socialist Republic), and he immediately set about using his position to undermine Gorbachev and the Union.

These developments persuaded the conservatives in Moscow to unite against the breakup of the Soviet Union. In the course of 1990–91 Gorbachev found himself fighting on two fronts, giving way first to the hard-liners, then veering toward the reformers. This zigzag course eventually led to the attempt by the hard-liners, still in control of the security forces, to stage a coup in August 1991, on the eve of the signing of a new Union Treaty, claiming Gorbachev vacationing in the Crimea had fallen ill and been replaced by his vice-president, one of the plotters. It was a breathless moment that might have resulted in bloody civil war, but in the event the plotters lost their nerve. Yeltsin was not only not arrested but didn't even have his telephone line cut.

Yeltsin made his headquarters in the Moscow White House, which had been completed in 1979 for the Russian Republic offices. A huge and sympathetic public gathered around the White House, making a living barrier around him and showing enormous public support. The hundreds of tanks brought into the capital by the five main coup plotters did not succeed in cowing the populace, who openly begged the soldiers to come over to the side of democracy. On the night of August 20, it was expected that the tanks would attack and that, if they did, they would easily take the White House. Nevertheless, the attack did not happen, although three young men lost their lives in forays against some tanks. On the third day, Gorbachev with his wife, Raisa, was brought back from the Crimea, where he had been under house arrest, his illness only an excuse for the plotters. The coup leaders were arrested.

Those few days were immensely significant. Yeltsin had gained the upper hand and held public confidence, not only in Moscow but also in all the major cities, where

WHITE HOUSE. In 1991 the White House was led by Russian President Boris Yeltsin (formerly Moscow Party Secretary). In August it became the focus of resistance to the attempted right-wing coup against the Gorbachev government. Despite swamping Moscow with tanks, the coup leaders were defeated. A few months later the Soviet Union collapsed, and Yeltsin found himself president of a new country, Russia. In 1993 tanks again were turned on the White House, when communists and hard-liners opposed to Yeltsin's reforms occupied the building. Some 150 people died in the subsequent disturbances.

everyone had watched the drama unfold on television. As leader, Gorbachev had been overtaken by events. He tried to regain the initiative by resigning as general secretary of the Communist Party and by convening a conference with the constituent members of the Soviet Union in the hope of preserving the Union in some form. But to no avail. The leaders of the republics were glad to have an opportunity for independence as a way of keeping themselves in power. By December 31 the Soviet Union ceased to exist, the hammer and sickle was lowered over the Kremlin, and the Russian Federation had come into being under President Boris Yeltsin.

Democracy and the New Russia

Yeltsin, so popular and admired for his courageous actions during the coup, appeared indecisive in the first few months, taking long vacations, and was unavailable when important decisions should have been made. Concerns were expressed over his health and drinking habits. However, in October he emerged to set the country on the path of radical reform, appointing in December the brilliant young economist, Yegor Gaidar. Soon after, Anatoly Chubais was given the task of introducing "privatization," the sale of state property, including apartments, to the individuals living in them for very little money. Thus for the first time since the revolution, Muscovites could legally have title to their own apartments. This was a popular move, but the sell-off of industrial enterprises was often accompanied by corruption and was perceived by the public as the impoverishment of the state to enrich the few.

Other reforms such as the lifting of price controls quickly caused prices to rise dramatically—in some cases by as much as 250 percent—and serious problems arose. Savings became almost valueless. Scarce food supplies suddenly became available but at prices impossible for most pockets, and public discontent was used by parliament under its leader, Khasbulatov, to attack the government. Gaidar was forced to resign in less than a year, and the pace of reform was slowed.

The struggle with parliament, now using the famous White House as their debating hall, continued to hinder Yeltsin and his advisers who were trying to push through reforms. The members of this parliament had been elected in Soviet times before the August coup and were mostly composed of hard-line communists and nationalists. In 1993 the conflict worsened. In March Yeltsin attempted to introduce emergency rule but watered the resolution down. In April he held a referendum for a new constitution that was overwhelmingly endorsed but failed to follow up his political advantage by decisive action. In September, in face of the continuing hostility of parliament, Yeltsin announced its dissolution. In October the parliamentarians led by Khasbulatov and Rutskoi, now calling himself acting president, fought back, refusing to leave the building. When they encouraged armed extremists among the demonstrators to take over key points in the city, including the mayor's office and the Ostankino television tower, fighting broke out. Yeltsin then ordered tanks to take up positions and fire against the White House, which withstood for several hours before the parliamentarians finally gave in. Khasbulatov and Rutskoi were arrested. 144 people died in this conflict.

The struggle between the hard-liners and Yeltsin continued to plague his government. In parliamentary elections in December 1993 Yeltsin's own party and others associated with it did unexpectedly poorly, so once more he had to govern with a hostile parliament, now known by its old name, the Duma. He was further frustrated when following a Duma resolution sponsored by his enemies, the coup plotters of August 1991 and Khasbulatov and Rutskoi were released in February 1994. Nevertheless, Yeltsin rallied after a bypass operation and unexpectedly won a large victory in the presidential election of 1996.

A further complication was the outbreak of violence in the republic of Chechnya in the Caucasus in 1994. The Chechens wanted to break away from Russia and were fomenting trouble in the border republics of Ingushetia and Dagestan. Russian troops sent in to quell the rebellion found themselves locked in a bloody conflict that attracted widespread international criticism. Russian forces mounted a major offensive in 1999, which reestablished Moscow's control, but guerrilla fighting continued.

Yeltsin's health, his notorious drinking habits, and his erratic behavior characterized the rest of his rule. He suddenly dismissed his popular and successful prime minister, Chernomyrdin, in the summer of 1998 and appointed a young, untried economist, Kirienko.

In August, as a result of the economic problems in Asia, the ruble suddenly fell sharply, precipitating an economic disaster. Kirienko was replaced by Primakov. However, in the end the Russian economy managed to weather the crisis remarkably well, those worst affected being the new rich businessmen.

In 1999 Yeltsin (whose health was worsening) began planning the succession. He dismissed Primakov and his successor Stepashin and appointed as prime minister the virtually unknown Vladimir Putin, a former KGB officer in East Germany. Yeltsin's sudden resignation at the end of 1999 gave Putin as acting president a head start in the presidential elections in March 2000, and he won convincingly. Following the atrocities in New York and Washington on September 11, 2001, Russia gave support to the United States in the battle against terrorism, which has led to improved relations between the two countries.

Given the terrible legacy of seventy-five years of communism, Russia has weathered the post-communist phase remarkably well, avoiding a bloody revolution or civil war, continuing to hold elections, able to keep its diverse regions together, and at last showing signs of economic recovery. For the ordinary Russians, the freedom to do and say as they wish after seven decades of totalitarian government is the most important change of all. Although there is a conscious attempt to give more power to the provinces, Moscow, at the center of this vast country, continues to be the most important city, the place where policies are formed and the fate of Russia is decided.

In 2002 Moscow gives the appearance of a boomtown, its population now nine million. Its formerly shabby old buildings in the center are shining with new paint and new well-designed office buildings are shooting up wherever there is space. New residential districts beginning to appear in the suburbs are no longer of high-rise towers but individual houses for the new wealthy entrepreneurs, a sign of the future. Many of the historical monuments that had been pulled down in Stalin's time are now rebuilt. The charming Kazan Cathedral in Red Square is back in place, the Iversky Gate closes off Red Square once more, and the Red Staircase in the Kremlin, personally rebuilt by Yeltsin, has reappeared once again linking the old palaces with the square.

A 1999 plan for the city was formulated by the charismatic Mayor Luzhkov, in which it was proposed to reduce by 25 percent the industrial zones of the city that lie near the historic heart. A third inner ring road is to be built, following the line of the inner circular railway, which should require a minimum amount of dislocation of older buildings. Within Moscow, the historic city is not to be threatened. The future at the beginning of the twenty-first century looks bright for Moscow.

RED SQUARE RENEWED. Kazan Cathedral, demolished in 1936, took its place again in November 1993 in Red Square across from the History Museum and the Nikolsky Gate of the Kremlin. It is a symbol of the renewed Moscow, which is acquiring a prosperous air as a result of the extravagant restoration and building projects of the energetic mayor, Yury Luzhkov.

BIBLIOGRAPHY

Berton, Kathleen. *Moscow: An Architectural History*. London: I. B. Tauris, 1990.

Buryshkin, Pavel Afanasevich. *Moskva Kupecheskaya*. Moscow: Stolitsa, 1990.

Colton, Timothy J. *Moscow: Governing the Socialist Metropolis*. Cambridge, MA: Belknap Press, 1996.

de Madariaga, Isabel. *Catherine the Great*. London: Yale University Press, 1990.

Fennell, J. L. I. *Ivan the Great of Moscow*. London: Macmillan, 1963.

Gorbachev, Mikhail. *Mikhail Gorbachev: Memoirs*. London: Bantam, 1997.

Graham, Stephen. *Ivan the Terrible*. North Haven, CT: Archon, 1968.

Hakluyt, Richard. *Voyages, 1589–99*. Vols. 1 & 2. London: Dent, 1962.

Hingley, Ronald. *The Tsars: Russian Autocrats 1533–1917*. London: Weidenfeld and Nicolson, 1968.

Hughes, Lindsey. *Russia in the Age of Peter the Great*. London: Yale University Press, 1998.

Kochan, Lionel, and John Keep. *The Making of Modern Russia.* London: Penguin, 1998.
Massie, Robert K. *Nicholas and Alexandra.* London: Victor Gollancz, 1968.
Murrell, Geoffrey. *Russia's Transition to Democracy.* Brighton, Sussex: Academic Press, 1997.
Murrell, Kathleen Berton. *Moscow Art Nouveau.* London: Philip Wilson, 1997.
———. *Russia.* New York: Alfred A. Knopf, 1998.
Romaniuk, Sergey. *Iz Istorii Moskovskikh Pereulkov.* Moscow: Svarog i K, 1998.
Rybakov, B. A. *Kievskaya Rus i Russkoe Knyazhestva XII–XIII vv.* Moscow: Nauka, 1993.
Sarabianov, Dmitry. *Russian Art from Neoclassicsm to the Avant-Garde 1800–1917.* London: Thames and Hudson, 1990.
Shmidt, S. O. ed. *Moskva Entsiklopediya.* Moscow: Bolshaya Rossiiskaya Entsiklopediya, 1997.
Sitwell, Sacheverell. *Valse des Fleurs.* London: Faber & Faber, 1941. Reprint. London: Sickle Moon Books, 2000.
Sytin, P. B. *Trudy Muzeya Istorii i Rekonstruktsii Moskvy.* Vols. 1 & 2. Moscow: Mosgorispolkoma, 1950, 1954.
Vernadsky, George. *A History of Russia.* New Haven, CT: Yale University Press, 1969.
Voyce, Arthur. *Moscow and the Roots of Russian Culture.* Newton Abbot, Devon, England: David and Charles, 1972.
Wilson, Francesca. *Muscovy, Russia through Foreign Eyes 1553–1900.* London: George Allen and Unwin, 1971.

INDEX

Note: Page numbers in *italics* indicate illustrations.

Abramov (writer), 186
Abramtsevo, 144–145
  bench by Mikhail Vrubel, *146*
Abuladze, Tengiz, 216–217
Academy of Sciences, 130
Acts of the Apostles, 42
adventurers, merchant, 42–43
A Journey from Petersburg to Moscow, 110
Akhmatova, Anna, 204
Alabyan (architect), 191–192
alcoholism, 112, 214
Alexander I, *114*
  and Decembrist conspirators, 124, 126
  education and start of reign, 115–116
  and 1812 memorial church, 133
  general information, 114
  and reconstruction of Moscow, 120–124
Alexander II
  assassination, 141
  and Decembrist conspirators, 129
  emancipation of serfs, 137–138
  reforms, 137–141
Alexander III, 141
Alexander III Museum, 149
Alexander Military School, 169
Alexander Nevsky, 23
Alexandra Palace, 130
Alexandra (wife of Nicholas II), 156, *156,* 164
Alexandrovich, Daniel, 22, 23
Alexandrovich, Yury, 23
Alexeevna, Catherine. *see* Catherine II, the Great
Alexis, the Most Gentle, 57–59, 61, 62, 63, 64, 69
Alexis (son of Nicholas II), *156,* 164
Alexis (son of Peter the Great), 77, 86
Allilueva, Nadezhda (wife of Stalin), 187
Ambrosy (Archbishop), 106, 108
Anastasia (daughter of Yaroslav the Wise), 17
Andropov, Yuri, 214

Anna (daughter of Yaroslav the Wise), 17
Anna Karenina, 133
anti-Semitism, 157, 159
Apraksin-Trubetskoy mansion, 94
aqueducts, 139
Arakcheev (Count), 116
architecture
art nouveau, 145, *147*
Ascension Church, *51*
Assumption Cathedral, *32*
Cathedral of Christ the Savior, 134, 135, *135*
Church of the Trinity, *67*
classical style, 102–103, 105–106
Cloudprop project, 190
constructivism, 192
destruction under Stalin, 189–190
eighteenth century, 80–83, 93–95, 100, 102–103, *104,* 105–106
empire style, 121–124, 130
Faceted Palace, *44, 71*
fifteenth century, 31–33, *32, 44*
Great Kremlin Palace, 134
Krasnye Vorota, 96, *96*
Krutitsky Podvore, 66
memorial church, 133–134
mid-seventeenth century, 65–67, *67*
mid-twentieth century, 191–193, 195, 209–210, *211*
Moorish-Gothic style, 103, *104*
Moscow baroque (Naryshkin), 73–74
neoclassicism, *151,* 161–162, *163,* 191
palace-estates, 105–106
Palace of Soviets, 195–196, *197*
Rastrelli and Ukhtomsky baroque, 93–95
reconstruction after fire, 120–124
reconstruction after World War II, 202–203
reconstruction under Stalin, 191
Red Army Building, 191
reforms of Patriarch Nikon, 60–61
Russo-Byzantine, 133–134, 135, 136
Savior in the Wood, 134, 136
seventeenth century, 50, 56–57, *57,* 64–66
Silver Age, 145
sixteenth century, 33–34, 51, *51*
St. Basil's Cathedral, 48, *48,* 49
Stalin Gothic style, 203–206
Terem Palace, *57, 71*
Trinity Cathedral, 27
twentieth century, 177–182, *179, 180*
twentieth century, early, 149, *150, 151*
utopianism, 190
wedding-cake towers, 203–204, *205*
wood vs. stone, 24–25, 56
art/artists
avant-garde, 148, 217
control under Stalin, 186, 204
effects of 1905 revolution, 161–162
eighteenth century, 110–111
under Gorbachev, 217

under Khrushchev, 208
new unions, 186
Plan of Monumental Propaganda, 177–178
during reign of Peter the Great, 80–83
Silver Age, 144–151
twentieth century, 177–182
Aurora battleship, 168–169
Avvakum (Archpriest of Old Believers), 61

Bakunin, Mikhail, 178
Balmont, Konstantin, 148
battle between Mongols and Russians, *21*
Battle of Friedland, 116
Battle of Kulikovo, 24, 92
Battle of Waterloo, 120
Battleship Potemkin, 159–160
Batu Khan, 20
Bazhenov, Vasily, 102–103, 105–106, 107
Bely, Andrey, 148
Beria, Lavrenty, 206
Bering, Vitus, 88
Big Three, 202
Biron, Ernst, 88
birth of Moscow, 18, 20
Black Square, 177
Blok, Alexander, 148
Blue Rose Group, 148
Bogolyubsky, Andrey, 17–18, 18
Bolshevik government
and civil war, 173–174
and destruction of monuments, 175
election of 1918, 170
Five-Year Plans, 185–186
Nazi-Soviet Pact, 198
New Economic Policy, 175–177
return of capital to Moscow, 170–171
Treaty of Brest-Litovsk, 173
War Communism, 175
Bolshevik Revolution, 168–169
Bolsheviks, 157–158, 166
Bolshoi Theater, 106, 121, *122*
Bonaparte, Napoleon, 116–120
Borisov-Musatov, Victor, 148
Bove, Osip, 121, 122
Boxer uprising (China), 158
Brezhnev, Leonid, 212–214
Bronze Horseman, The, 84
Bruce, James, 81
Bryusov, Valery, 148
bubonic plague, 40
Butovo massacres and memorials, 188, *188*

Cameron, Charles, 102
cannibalism, 186
Catherine I (second wife of Peter the Great), 86
Catherine II, the Great, *99*
architectural projects, 100, 102–103, *104,* 105–106
coup d'etat, 98, 100
and literature, 110–111
marriage to Peter III, 95, 97–98
Catherine Palace, 94
cavalry school, 124, *125*
censorship
under Brezhnev, 212, 213
during the Cold War, 203
under Nicholas I, 130–131
under Stalin, 186
twentieth century, 155

Chagall, Marc, 148, 177
Chancellor, Richard, 42–43, 46–47
Charles XII (King of Sweden), 78, 79
Chechnya, 223
Chekhov, Anton, 133
Chernenko, Konstantin, 214
Chernobyl nuclear explosion, 216
Chernomyrdin, Viktor, 223
Chernyshev family, 124
children, homeless, 176–177
Children of the Arbat, 216
cholera, 130
chronology of events, 1–9
Chubais, Anatoly, 221
churches/cathedrals. *see also* monasteries/convents
  Annunciation Cathedral, 33
  Archangel Michael Cathedral, 33
  architectural reforms, 60–61
  Ascension Church, 51, *51*
  Assumption Cathedral, 31–33, *32*
  Byzantine, 15, *16*
  Cathedral of Christ the Savior, 134, 135, *135,* 196
  Cathedral Square, 31
  Church of the Savior Untouched by Hand, 145
  Church of the Savior *v Boru,* 25
  Church of Sts. Peter and Paul, 82, *82*
  Church of the Trinity, 65–67, *67*
  churches-under-the-bells, 74
  Deposition of the Robe Church, 33
  destruction under Stalin, 189–190
  eleventh century, 15
  Great Ascension Church, 216
  Intercession at Fili, 74
  Kazan Cathedral, 225, *226*
  memorial church, 133–134
  Menshikov Tower, 80
  Moscow baroque (Naryshkin), 73–74
  parish churches, 65
  reopening and repair, 215–216, 217
  Savior Cathedral, 26, *26*
  Savior in the Wood, 134, 136
  St. Basil's Cathedral, 48, *48,* 49
  St. Nikita the Martyr, 95
  St. Sophia of Novgorod, 15, 16, *16*
  Trinity Cathedral, 27
Churchill, Winston, 202
civil war, 173–174
Cold War, 202–206
collapse of Soviet power, 217–219, 221
Commission for the Construction of Moscow, 121
communal apartments, 174
Company of Merchant Adventurers, 42
concentration camps, 187, 203, 206
Congress of Vienna, 120
Constantine (brother of Alexander I), 126
convents. *see* monasteries/convents
Cossacks, 46, 63–64
Crimean War, 113, 136–137
Crusades, 17
Cuban missile crisis, 209

Cumans, 17
Cyril, Saint, 15

d'Anthes, Baron, 131
Dashkova, Catherine, 98
Dead Souls, 132
Decembrist conspiracy, 124–127, 129
decline and abandonment of Moscow, 83–84
destruction of Moscow, 117, *119,* 119–120
Dictatorship of Conscience, 217
Djugashvili, Joseph. *see* Stalin, Joseph
Dmitry (son of Ivan IV), 52–53
Dolgorukov, Catherine, 87
Dolgorukov mansion, 106
Dolgoruky, Yury, 18, *19*
Donkey's Tail, 148
Donskoy, Dmitry. *see* Ivanovich, Dmitry (Donskoy)
Dostoevsky, Fedor, 131, 132
Dr. Zhivago, 208
Dudintsev, Vladimir, 206

economy
  and alcoholism, 112
  customs dues and control of illegal goods, 89
  and Gorbachev reforms, 214–217
  industrial growth, eighteenth century, 111–112
  under Ivan IV, 41
  New Economic Policy, 176–177
  nineteenth century, 113
  ruble, value of, 223
  twentieth century, early, 158
  and Yeltsin reforms, 222
education
  discrimination under Stalin, 186
  reforms under Alexander II, 138, 139
  twentieth century, early, 149
Ehrenburg, Ilya, 206
Eisenstein, Sergei Mikhailovich, 160
Elizabeth (daughter of Peter the Great), 79, 89–94, *90*
Elizabeth (daughter of Yaroslav the Wise), 17
Elizabeth I (Queen of England), 43
El Lissitsky, 190
emigration
  of eastern Slavs to Moscow, 18
  of Slavic tribes, 13
empresses and law of succession, 85–86
English Embassy, 45, *45*
epidemics
  bubonic plague, 40, 106, 108
  cholera, 130
Evelyn, John, 76

Faceted Palace, 33–34, 44, *44*
False Dmitry's, 53–54
Fedor (half brother of Peter the Great), 69
Fedor (son of Ivan IV), 52
Fioraventi, Alberti, 31
fire of Moscow, 117, *119,* 119–120
First Revolution, 159–161
Foreigners' Settlement, 58, 72, 93
foreign influence, 58–59
freedom of expression, 186
freedom of the press, 160
freedom of speech, 224

freedom of thought, 131
French invasion, 116–117, 119–120

Gagarin, Yury, 208
Gaidar, Yegor, 221, 222
Galloway, Christopher, 35
geography, 11–12
German invasion, 199–202
Ghengis Khan, 21
Gida (wife of Yury Dolgoruky), 18
Girey, Devlet, 40
glasnost (greater openness), 215
Godunov, Boris, 52–54
Gogol, Nikolay, 132
Golden Horde. *see* Mongols
Golitsyn, Mikhail, 88
Golitsyn, Vasily, 72
Goncharova, Natalya, 148
Gorbachev, Mikhail, 214–221
Gorbachev, Raisa, 219
Gordon, Patrick, 75, 77
Gorky, Maxim, 147, 169
government. *see also* Bolshevik government
  attempted coup of 1991, 219, 220
  collapse of Soviet power, 217–219, 221
  collective leadership (first), 206–207
  collective leadership (second), 212
  corruption and nepotism, 213
  democracy, 221–225
  de-Stalinization process, 206–210
  election of 1918, 170
  Helsinki Agreement, 212
  justice system reforms, 139–140
  local (zemstvo) councils, 138–139
  Marxist political groups, 166
  Petrograd soviet, 165–166
  political opposition groups, 155, 157–158
  political parties, 207
  Provisional Government, 165–166, 168, 169
  radical political groups, 157–158
  reforms of Alexander II, 138–141
  reforms of Yeltsin, 221–222
  SALT 1 agreement, 212
  state Dumas, 160, 161
  Third Department, 131
Great Kremlin Palace, 134
Great Northern War, 79
Great Purge, 187, 188
Great Terror, 187
Grishin, Victor, 215
Guards Regiments, 98, 101
Gulag Archipelago, The, 213
GUM, 149, 150, *150*. *see also* Upper Trading Rows.

Hakluyt, Richard, 46–47
Hall of Columns, 106
Hastie, William, 121
Hastings, Mary, 43
health
  bubonic plague, 40, 106, 108
  cholera, 130
healthcare, 138, 139
Helsinki Agreement, 212
Hermitage Museum, 94
Hero of Our Time, 132
History Museum, 149

History of Russia, 111
Hotel Ukraine, *205*
housing
  late 1950s, 210
  1960s–1980s, 210, *211*
  twentieth century, 174, 178, *179,* 181
twenty-first century, 224
Hypatian Chronicle
  on Dolgoruky, 18, 19

Industrial Revolution, 141–142, 144
industry
  agriculture, 111–112, 116, 185–186, 207–208
  corruption, 213
  effects of emancipation, 141
  labor strikes, 159–161, 162–163, 164, 165
  manufacturing, 111
  mining, 111
  science and technology, 142, 144
  textile, 111, 141–142
  transportation, 136, 144
Inspector-General, 132
Institute of Aerodynamics, 144
intellectuals/intelligentsia
  influence on Alexander II, 137
  Land and Freedom organization, 140
  People's Will, 140–141
  self-publishing of literature, 213
  Slavophiles, 130, 140
  Westernizers, 130
Ivan (half brother of Peter the Great), 69, 70, 74
Ivan (son of Ivan IV), 52
Ivan II "Krasny," the Handsome, 23
Ivan III, the Great, 27–28
Ivan IV, the Terrible, *39*
  achievements of, 42–43
  beginning of reign, 37–38
  description by Richard Chancellor, 47
  division of the kingdom, 38, 40
  economy under, 41
  and Siberian exploration, 46
  sixteenth-century Moscow, 46–50, 52
Ivan VI (grandnephew of Empress Anna), 89
Ivan "Kalita," moneybags, 23
Ivanovich, Dmitry (Donskoy), 24
Ivanovna, Anna, 87–88
Iversky Gate, 225

Jewish community, 157, 159
July Days, 168

Kaganovich, Lazar, 191
Kandinsky, Vasily, 148, 177
Kazakov, Matvey, 102, 103, 105, 106, 123
Kennedy, John F., 209
Kerensky, Alexander, 165–166
KGB, 214
Khasbulatov, Ruslan, 222, 223
Khmelnitsky, Hetman Bogdan, 64
Khodynka Field, 157
Khovansky (streltsy leader), 72
Khrushchev, Nikita, 191, 206–209
Kiev
  effect of Crusades, 17
  effect of Cumans, 17

fall of, 17–18
tenth and eleventh centuries, 15, 17
Treaty of Andrussovo, 64
Kiev Academy, 81
killing fields, 187, *188*
Kirienko (prime minister), 223
Kirov, Sergey, 187
Kon, Fedor, 50
Kraft, Alexander, 177
Krasnye Vorota, 96, *96*
Kremlin
architectural redesign, 102–103
aerial view, *36*
under Bolshevik government, 171
as a fortress, 65
Great Kremlin Palace, 134
Poteshny Palace, 172, *172*
reconstruction and expansion under Ivan III, 28–35
Spassky Gate, 35, *35*
streltsy guards, 70, 72, 75, 76–77, 81
view from the Moskva River, *29*
Krupskaya (wife of Vladimir Lenin), 170
Krutitsky Podvore, 66
Kutuzov (Marshal), 117
Kuznetsov, Pavel, 148

labor, child, 177
labor movement, 140. *see also* industry
labor unions, 159–161
LaHarpe (tutor of Alexander I), 115
Larionov, Mikhail, 148
Lefort, Franz, 75, 77
Lenin, Vladimir, *167*
death of, 183
destruction of monuments, 175
escape to Finland, 168
last testament/memoranda, 183
New Economic Policy, 175–177
Plan of Monumental Propaganda, 177–178
political start, 157
return from Finland as Bolshevik leader, 170–171
return from Switzerland after Revolution, 166
War Communism, 175
Leningrad, 183
Lenin mausoleum, 184, *184*
Lermontov, Mikhail, 132
Life, 61
literacy, 15, 149
literature
after Stalin's death, 206
under Brezhnev, 212, 213
and Catherine the Great, 110–111
during the Cold War, 204
and first printing press, 42
and freedom of the press, 160
under Khrushchev, 208
Moskovskie Vedomosti (Moscow Gazette), 93
nineteenth century, 131–133
Novaya Zhizn (New Life), 169
seventeenth century, 61
twelfth century, 15, 17
twentieth century, early, 148
twentieth century, late, 216
Lomonosov, Mikhail, 93, 111
Lopukhina, Yevdokiya (wife of Peter the Great), 74, 77

Louis XV (of France), 79
Lunacharsky, Anatoly, 169
Luzhkov, Yuri, 225, 226
Lvov, Georgy, 165
Lysenko, Trofim, 208

Maddox, Michael, 106
Malenkov, Georgy, 206
Malevich, Kazimir, 148, 177
Mamontov, Savva, 144
maps
  Boulevard Ring, *x, xi*
  Kremlin, *36*
  Muscovy (Moscow) 1598, *30*
  Russia before 1917, *152–153*
march across the Alps, 116
march on Russia by Napoleon, 116–117
Marshall Plan, 203
Marxism, 157, 166
Mathematical and Navigational School, 81
Matveev, Artamon, 69, 70
media, 216
Melnikov, Konstantin, 180, 181–182
Melnikov House, 180, *180,* 181
Mensheviks, 158, 166
Menshikov, Alexander, 86
merchant-adventurers, 42–43, 46–47
Methodius, Saint, 15
metro stations, 193, *193,* 195, 204
Michael (brother of Nicholas II), 165
Michurin, Ivan, 89
Mikhailov, Peter, 76
Mikhailov Castle, 115
military
  army, 78–80
  Izmailovsky regiment, 98
  naval fleet, 73, 75, 76, 78, 158–159
  Preobrazhensky regiment, 72, 98
  replacement of streltsy, 81
  secret societies, 124
  Semenovsky regiment, 72, 98
Miloslavskaya, Mariya (wife of Peter the Great), 69
Minin, Kozma, 54
Molotov, Vyacheslav Mikhailovich, 198
monarchy, 85–86
monasteries/convents. *see also* churches/cathedrals
  Alexeevsky Monastery, 50
  Andronikov Monastery, 25, 26, *26*
  Chudov Monastery, 25
  Danilov Monastery, 25, 217
  destruction under Stalin, 189–190
  Donskoy Monastery, 50, 52
  New Jerusalem Resurrection Monastery, 61–63, *62*
  Novodevichy Convent, 50, 52, 74, 77
  Novospassky Monastery, 50, 52
  Resurrection Monastery, 202–203
  Rozhdestvensky Monastery, 25, 50
  Simonov Monastery, 25
  Smolny Convent, 94
  Sretensky Monastery, 25, 50

Trinity-St. Sergius Monastery, 27, 74–75, 92, *92*, 95
Voznesensky Monastery, 25
Vysokopetrovsky Monastery, 25, 50
Mongols
Battle of Kulikovo, 24
colonization, 22–24
invasion by, 20, *21*, 22
and the Russian Orthodox Church, 23–24
tribute gatherers, 23
tribute to, 20–21, 23
Monomakh, Vladimir, 18
monument at Borodino, 118, *118*
monuments
destruction by Lenin, 175
rebuilding in the twenty-first century, 224–225
Monument to the Third International, 178
Morozov, Savva, 142
Morozov, Savva (grandson), 142, 143
Morozov, Timofei, 140
Moscow Art Theater, *143*
Moscow Commission, 121
Moscow News, 216
Moscow rebellion, 108
Moscow University, 111, 123, *123*
Moskovskie Vedomosti (Moscow Gazette), 93
Moskva Hotel, 192, *192*
Moskva River, 22
Muraviev, Nikolay, 124
Murrell, Geoffrey, 129, 132
Museum of Architecture, 178
museums, 94, 149, 178
music/musicians
during the Cold War, 204
twentieth century, early, 145, 148

Naryshkin, Lev, 74
Naryshkina, Natalya, 69
Navigational School. *see* Mathematical and Navigational School
Nevsky, Alexander, 22–23
New Economic Policy, 175–177
Nicholas I, the Stick, 126, 129–137
Nicholas II
beginning of reign, 157
discrimination and anti-Semitism, 157
family portrait, *156*
October Manifesto, 160
and Revolution of 1905, 159–161
and World War I, 164
Nikitnikov, Grigory, 66
Nikon, Patriarch, 50, 59–63, 202
Noble's Club, 106
Not by Bread Alone, 206
Novaya Zhizn (New Life), 169
Novi, Alevisio, 33
Novikov, Nikolay, 111
Novy Mir, 216

obelisk to the Soviet constitution, 178
October Manifesto, 160
Ogurtsov, Bazhen, 35
Olga (Grand Duchess), 15
oligarchy, 85, 87
Olympic Games, 212–213

One Day in the Life of Ivan Denisovich, 208
oppression, 155
Oprichnina, 40, 52
Orlov, Alexis, 98–99
Orlov, Grigory, 97–98, 108
Orlov, Vladimir, 101
Orlov brothers, 100, 101
Ostashevo, 125, *125*

Palace of Soviets, 134, 195–196, *197*
Pale of Settlement, 157
Paleologus, Sophia (wife of Ivan III), 28
Panin (Count), 137
Pashkov House, 103, 106, 107, *107*
Pasternak, Boris, 208
Paul I (son of Catherine the Great), 110, 111, 115
Peace of Tilsit, 116
peasants/peasantry
  collectivization of agriculture, 185–186
  discrimination and oppression, 155
  emancipation of serfs, 137–138
  and government reforms, 139
  rebellion led by Stenka Razin, 59
  and rebellions, 108–110
  serfdom, 41
perestroika (restructuring), 215–219
Peter, Metropolitan, 23, 25
Peter (grandson of Peter the Great), 86–87
Peter (son of Alexis the Most Gentle), 58–59
Peter the Great, *68*
  arts and architecture, 80–83
  childhood, 72–73
  construction of St. Petersburg, 83–84
  co-rulers, 70, 72
  coup attempt by streltsy, 76–77
  general information, 68, 69
  marriage of, 74
  military reformation, 78–80
  new law of succession, 85–86
  shipbuilding and naval fleet, 73, 76, 78
  as sole ruler, 74–75
  Western influence on, 75–78
Peter III, 95, 97, 98, 100
Peter Travel Palace, 103
Petrashevsky Circle, 131
Philaret (father of Michael Romanov), 55, 56
plague, 40, 106, 108
Plekhanov, Georgy, 157
Polish invasion, 54, 56
political radicals, 124–127, 129
political repression, 113
pollution, 215
Popova, Lyubov, 148
population
  during Bolshevik government, 174
  in the 1960s, 210
  in 1935, 191
  in the 1700s, 105
  seventeenth century, 64
  twentieth century, early, 148, 158
  in 2002, 224
Potemkin, 160
Potemkin, Grigory, 100

Pozharsky (Russian prince), 54
Preobrazhensky Palace, 72, 74, 77
Primakov (prime minister),
223, 224
Primary Chronicle
on the Byzantine Church, 15
on invitation to Norsemen, 14
primogeniture, 115. *see also*
monarchy
Principal Navigations, Voyages, Traffics and Discoveries, 46–47
printing press, 42
Prokofiev, Lina, 204
Prokofiev, Sergey, 23, 204
propaganda, 173, 177–178
Pugachev, Emelyan, 109
Pugachev Rebellion, 109–110
Pushkin, Alexander, 84, 127,
128, *128,* 131, 132
Pushkin Museum, 149
Putin, Vladimir, 224

Quarenghi, Giacomo, 102

Radishchev, Alexander, 110
Rasputin, Grigory, 156, 164
Rastrelli, Bartolomeo, 88, 93–95
Razin, Stenka, 59
Razumovsky, Alexis, 93
rebellions, 108, 109–110
reconstruction of Moscow
after the fire and French
invasion, 120–124
after the revolution, 190–195
after World War II, 202–203
Red Army, 173
Red Guards, 169
Red Square, 25, 49, *201,* 225, *226*
Red Staircase, 71, *71,* 225
reforms
of Alexander II, 137–141
under Gorbachev, 214–217
of Yeltsin, 221–222
religion/religious
Bogolyubsky Virgin icon,
kissing of, 106, 108
Crusades, 17
foreign influence on, 58–59
formation of Uniate Church, 63
Holy Synod, 189
icons, 24, 25, 27, 31–33
Mongol tolerance of
Orthodoxy, 24
office of patriarch, 189
Old Believers, 61, 72, 145, 157
persecution, 61, 72, 157
reforms of Patriarch Nikon,
59–63
Russian Orthodox Church,
23–24
schism in the church, 59–61, 62
Virgin of Vladimir, 24, 32
Repentance, 216–217
Revolution of 1905, 159–161
Revolutions of 1917, 165–170
Ribbentrop, Joachim von, 198
rivers and tributaries, 22
Romanov, Michael, 54–56, *55,* 58
Roosevelt, Franklin D., 202
Rostopchin (Count), 117
Royal Palace at Uglich, *53*
Rublev, Andrey, 25–27
Ruffo, Marco, 34
Rules of the Five Orders, The, 81
Rumyantsev Museum, 149
Rurik (Varangian/Viking
prince), 14
Russian expansion, 136–137

Russian Revolution, 165–170
Russian Social Democratic Labor Party (RSDLP), 157
Rutskoi, Aleksandr, 222, 223
Ryabushinsky, Dmitry, 144
Ryabushinsky, Stepan, 145
Ryabushinsky House, *147*
Rybakov, Anatoly, 216

SALT 1 agreement, 212
Saltykov, Sergey, 97, 108
school of architecture, 95
science, eighteenth century, 110–111
Scriabin, Alexander, 148
secret police, 187, 214
secret societies, 103, 124
Semenovskoe, 100, *101*
serfdom, 41, 108–110, 113, 137–138
Seven Years' War, 95
Shakhovskoy family, 124
Shatrov, Mikhail, 217
Shatsky's Settlement School, 149
Shchusev, Alexei, 181, 184, 192, 202
Shekhtel, Fedor, 143, 145, 147
Sheremetiev family, 124
shipbuilding, 76
Shostakovich, Dmitry, 204
Shuisky, 54
Shuvalov, Ivan, 93
Siberian exploration, 46
Silver Age, 144–151
Sitwell, Sacheverell, 84
sixteenth-century Moscow, 46–54
slavery. *see* serfdom
Slavic tribes, emigration, 13
Slavonic-Greek-Latin Academy, 81
Smolny Institute, 168
Social Revolutionaries, 166
Sokol Garden Suburb, 179, *179,* 181
Solario, Antonio, 34
Solzhenitsyn, Alexander, 203, 208, 213
Song of Igor's Campaign, The, 15, 17
Sophia (half sister of Peter the Great), 70, 72, 74, 75, 77
Sophia of Anhalt-Zerbst. *see* Catherine II, the Great
Spaso House, 163, *163*
Spassky Gate, 35, *35*
St. Petersburg/Petrograd, 83
St. Sophia of Novgorod, 15, 16, *16*
stables at Ostashevo, 125, *125*
Stalin, Joseph
  and the Cold War, 202–206
  death, 204
  and Doctors' Plot fabrication, 204
  Five-Year Plans, 185–186
  and German invasion, 198–202
  the Great Purge, 187, 188
  and the Moscow-Volga canal, 194, *194,* 195
  Nazi-Soviet Pact, 198
  and Palace of Soviets, 134
  reburial, 209
  residency after Bolshevik takeover, 171
  rise to power, 183, 185–186
  Yalta Conference, 202
Stanislavsky, Konstantin, 144
Stepanova, Varvara, 148

Stepashin (prime minister), 224
Stolypin, Pyotr, 161
streltsy, Kremlin guards, 70, 72, 75, 76–77, 81
Sukharev Tower, 81
Susanna. *see* Sophia (half sister of Peter the Great)
Suvorov (General), 116
Svyatoslav (Varangian/Viking prince), 14

Tamerlane (Mongol/Tatar leader), 24
Tatars. *see* Mongols
Tatishchev, Vasily, 110
Tatlin, Vladimir, 178
Tatlin Tower, 178
Tchaikovsky, Peter Ilich, 145, 148
Terem Palace, 56–57, *57*
territorial expansion, 63–64
Thaw, The, 206
theater, 106, 216–217
Theater Square, 121
Third Department, 131
Tikhon, Patriarch, 189
Time of Troubles, 52–66
Tolstoy, Lev, 132–133, 141
Ton, Konstantin, 133–134, 135
trade routes/trade, 14, 22, 42–43, 158
trade unions, 159–161
transportation
  air travel, 144
  and government reforms, 139
  metro stations, 193, *193,* 195, 200, 204
  Moscow-Volga canal, 194, *194,* 195
  railway, 136, 144, 158, 173
  roadways, 210, 225
Treaty of Andrussovo, 64
Treaty of Brest-Litovsk, 173
treaty with China, 72
Tretyakov Gallery, 149
tribute
  Ivan III's challenge of, 28
  to Mongols, 20–21, 23
  and Moscow princes as gatherers, 23
  to Norse princes, 14
Triple Entente, 162
Trotsky, Leon, 160, 166, *167,* 168, 171, 173, 185
Trubetskaya, Mariya, 129
Trubetskoy, Sergey, 129
Tsaritsyno, 103, *104*
Turgeniev, Ivan, 132
Tyurin, Yevgraf, 130

Ukhtomsky, Dmitry, 95
Ukraine, 64
Ulyanov, Vladimir. *see* Lenin, Vladimir
Upper Trading Rows, 149
Uvarov, Sergey, 130

Valse des Fleurs, 84
Vasily I (son of Dmitry Ivanovich), 27
Vasily II (son of Vasily I), 27
Vasily III (son of Ivan III), 37
Victory Day 1945, 201, *201*
Vignola, Giacomo, 81
Viking (Varangian) Norsemen, arrival, 14
Virgin of Vladimir, 24
Vitberg, Alexander, 133

Vladimir, town of, 18
Vladimir I, 15
Volkonskaya, Zinaida, 127, 129
Vrubel, Mikhail, 145, 146
Vtorov, Nikolay, 163

War Communism, 175
War and Peace, 133
White House, 219, 220, *220*
Whites, 169, 173
William (King of England), 76
Willoughby, Hugh, 42
Winter Palace, 94
Witte, Sergey, 160
workers' clubs, 180
World War I, 162–164
World War II, 198–202
Wright, Frank Lloyd, 195
writers
  after Stalin's death, 206
  under Brezhnev, 212, 213
  during the Cold War, 204
  under Khrushchev, 208
  late twentieth century, 216
  nineteenth century, 131–133
  seventeenth century, 61
  twentieth century, early, 148

Yalta Conference, 202
Yaroslav the Wise, 17
Yelena (mother of Ivan IV), 37
Yeltsin, Boris, 215, 218, 219–224
Yermak (Cossack leader), 46
Yevgeny Onegin, 132
Yury (son of Dmitry Ivanovich), 27

Zaikov, Lev, 216
Zakharina, Anastasia (wife of Ivan IV), 38
Zemshchina, 40
Zemsky Sobor, 42, 52, 56
Zemtsov, Mikhail, 89
Zhdanov, Andrey, 204
Zhukovsky, Nikolay, 142, 144
Zhukovsky air academy, 208
Zoshchenko (writer), 204